YONFAN'S
Bugis Street

T0345752

The New Hong Kong Cinema series

The New Hong Kong Cinema came into existence under very special circumstances, during a period of social and political crisis resulting in a change of cultural paradigms. Such critical moments have produced the cinematic achievements of the early Soviet cinema, neorealism, the *nouvelle vague*, and the German cinema of the 1970s and, we can now say, the New Hong Kong Cinema. If this cinema grew increasingly intriguing in the 1980s, after the announcement of Hong Kong's return to China, it is largely because it had to confront a new cultural and political space that was both complex and hard to define, where the problems of colonialism were uncannily overlaid with those of globalism. Such uncanniness could not be caught through straight documentary or conventional history writing: it was left to the cinema to define it.

Has the creative period of the New Hong Kong Cinema now come to an end? However we answer the question, there is a need to evaluate the achievements of Hong Kong cinema. This series distinguishes itself from the other books on the subject by focusing in-depth on individual Hong Kong films, which together make the New Hong Kong Cinema.

Series General Editors

Ackbar Abbas, Wimal Dissanayake, Mette Hjort, Gina Marchetti, and Stephen Teo

Series Advisors

Chris Berry, Nick Browne, Ann Hui, Leo Lee, Li Cheuk-to, Patricia Mellencamp, Meaghan Morris, Paul Willemen, Peter Wollen, and Wu Hung

✦ ✦ ✦ ✦ ✦

YONFAN'S
Bugis Street

Kenneth Chan

HKU
PRESS
香港大學出版社

Hong Kong University Press
The University of Hong Kong
Pokfulam Road
Hong Kong
www.hkupress.org

ISBN 978-988-8208-75-3 (*Paperback*)
ISBN 978-988-8208-76-0 (*Hardback*)

British Library Cataloguing-in-Publication Data
A catalogue record for this book is available from the British Library.

10 9 8 7 6 5 4 3 2 1

Printed and bound by CTPS Digiprints Ltd. in Hong Kong, China

Contents

Series Preface

The New Hong Kong cinema came into existence under very special circumstances, during a period of social and political crisis resulting in a change of cultural paradigms. Such critical moments have produced the cinematic achievements of the early Soviet cinema, neorealism, the *nouvelle vague*, the German cinema in the 1970s and, we can now say, the recent Hong Kong cinema. If this cinema grew increasingly intriguing in the 1980s, after the announcement of Hong Kong's return to China, it was largely because it had to confront a new cultural and political space that was both complex and hard to define, where the problems of colonialism were overlaid with those of globalism in an uncanny way. Such uncanniness could not be caught through straight documentary or conventional history writing; it was left to the cinema to define it.

It does so by presenting to us an urban space that slips away if we try to grasp it too directly, a space that cinema coaxes into existence by whatever means at its disposal. Thus it is by eschewing a narrow idea of relevance and pursuing disreputable genres like melodrama, kung fu and the fantastic that cinema brings into view something else about the city which could otherwise be missed. One classic example is Stanley Kwan's *Rouge*, which draws on the unrealistic form of the ghost story to evoke something of the uncanniness of Hong Kong's urban space. It takes a ghost to catch a ghost.

In the new Hong Kong cinema, then, it is neither the subject matter nor a particular set of generic conventions that is paramount. In fact, many Hong Kong films begin by following generic conventions but proceed to transform them. Such transformation of genre is also the transformation of a sense of place where all the rules have quietly and deceptively changed. It is this shifting sense of place, often expressed negatively and indirectly—but in the best work always rendered precisely in (necessarily) innovative images—that is decisive for the New Hong Kong Cinema.

Has the creative period of the New Hong Kong Cinema come to an end? However we answer the question, there is a need now to evaluate the achievements of Hong Kong cinema. During the last few years, a number of full-length books have appeared, testifying to the topicality of the subject. These books survey the field with varying degrees of success, but there is yet an almost complete lack of authoritative texts focusing in depth on individual Hong Kong films. This book series on the New Hong Kong Cinema is designed to fill this lack. Each volume will be written by a scholar/critic who will analyse each chosen film in detail and provide a critical apparatus for further discussion including filmography and bibliography.

Our objective is to produce a set of interactional and provocative readings that would make a self-aware intervention into modern Hong Kong culture. We advocate no one theoretical position; the authors will approach their chosen films from their own distinct points of vantage and interest. The aim of the series is to generate open-ended discussions of the selected films, employing diverse analytical strategies, in order to urge the readers towards self-reflective engagements with the films in particular and the Hong Kong cultural space in general. It is our hope that this series will contribute to the sharpening of Hong Kong culture's conceptions of itself.

In keeping with our conviction that film is not a self-enclosed signification system but an important cultural practice among similar others, we wish to explore how films both reflect and inflect culture. And it is useful to keep in mind that reflection of reality and reality of reflection are equally important in the understanding of cinema.

Ackbar Abbas
Wimal Dissanayake

Acknowledgments

Yonfan's Bugis Street is a book of transoceanic productivity. Personally, I would have found it much harder to write this book if I had remained in Singapore. In other words, the physical distance from my original homeland has granted me the critical space I needed to bring this work to fruition. But, the luxury of diasporic distance should not blind one to the material, technological, institutional, social, and cultural networks that serve as the foundation for research projects in an age of global mobility. Funding from various organizations has enabled me to shuttle between the United States and a number of locations for research and conference purposes, including Exeter, Amsterdam, Taipei, and, of course, Singapore. As one of the seven network partners of the project "Chinese Cinemas in the 21st Century: Production, Consumption, Imagination," I am grateful to the Leverhulme Trust for funding the network project and to Song Hwee Lim, the project's principal investigator, for generously bringing me into the network. My home institution, the University of Northern Colorado, has also provided grant funding through the Provost Research, Dissemination, and Faculty Development program, with additional travel support from the College of Humanities and Social Sciences. The Faculty Reassignment Award for Research, Scholarship, and Creative Works further relieved me of some teaching duties so that I could focus on completing the book manuscript. Much of the research material support I owe to the University of Northern Colorado's Michener Library, especially the unstinting efforts of Gregory Heald and Andrea Falcone. Of particular help on the Singapore end are the National Archives of Singapore, the National Heritage Board, the National Library Board, and the Asian Film Archive (AFA). I want to thank specifically Karen Chan of the AFA for helping me source material on queer Singapore cinema and for organizing the 2013 public talk on Yonfan's film at the FilmGarde Cineplex located near the geographical Bugis Street. Maggie Lye, one of the actresses in the film whom I got to meet at this public talk, was extremely generous in sharing her experiences and in providing me newspaper clippings from the 1990s. My graduate assistant Nathan Fuhr was tireless and much more creative than I was in identifying primary and critical works of importance to my project. To shore up my subpar language abilities, Ting-Kai Su shared his linguistic and translation skills by patiently working through Chinese-language texts with me, for which I am immeasurably grateful. The editorial and production staff of Hong Kong University Press, especially Christy Leung, Eric Mok, and Sherlon Ip, have been a pleasure to work with. I also appreciate the intellectually stimulating comments and useful suggestions from the reviewers of my book proposal and manuscript, which I believe has helped make this a much better book than it was originally conceived. And, finally, I am deeply grateful to director Yonfan for his generous professional support, especially in sharing useful research material and in granting the press permission to use a still from his film to grace the cover of this book.

My colleagues (in the areas of Chinese and Asian cinema and cultural studies) and the friends I have made as a result of my professional connections have been invaluable in their encouragement and intellectual support. I want to thank, particularly, Chris Berry, Michelle Bloom, Brenda Chan, Evans Chan, Rey Chow, Guo-Juin Hong, Earl Jackson, Gaik Cheng Khoo, Olivia Khoo, Jeroen de Kleot, Helen Hok-Sze Leung, Liew Kai Khiun, Kien Ket Lim, Shirley Geok-lin Lim, Song Hwee Lim, Gina Marchetti, Jim Straker, Julian Stringer, Andrew Stuckey, Stephen Teo, Yiman Wang, James Wren, and Audrey Yue. The faculty and staff of the Department of English and of the College of Humanities and Social Sciences at the University of Northern Colorado have generously urged me to pursue my research agenda and have provided collegial and material support. I am especially grateful to Brenda Cozzens, Marcus Embry, Lahcen Ezzaher, Joonok Huh, Karen Janata, Jeraldine Kraver, Michelle Low, Norm Peercy, José Suárez, Ben Varner, Lloyd Worley, and Lisa Zimmerman. I also want to acknowledge friends who have helped make Colorado home for me, thus diminishing the loneliness that is scholarly research: Mary Angeline, Richard Goldfarb, Gordon Harrison (my figure-skating coach), Larry Kinnison, and Kim McEntire. I am, as always, indebted to my extended family, to Virgil Mooneyhan, and to my parents Edward and Lily Chan. Finally, this book would not have been possible without my partner, David Mooneyhan, who has patiently and lovingly seen me through the project from start to finish.

Introduction

Bugis Street as Historical-Political-Cultural Discourse

Bugis Street and Cultural Anxiety

The mere mention of *Bugis Street* (1995) evokes fascinatingly awkward responses, especially among cinema audiences who are familiar with Yonfan's film. So, to begin my book-length analysis of this Hong Kong-Singapore work, I want to reflect upon *Bugis Street* as a cinematic text of cultural anxiety. While it is true that one can isolate moments of cultural and political anxieties in its narrative and thematic foci, I am instead interested here in the film's cultural reception and, consequently, how that response has an impact on the way scholarly critical work on the film is perceived. Allow me to approach this matter, rather unscientifically, by way of a personal anecdote. When I began describing to friends and family members in Singapore that I was working on a project about Yonfan's *Bugis Street*, a common response was one of, first, incredulous bemusement, which was then often accompanied by an involuntary rolling of eyes or a tepid offering of obligatory support marked contradictorily by condescending indulgence. In fact, even some of my academic colleagues in Asian film studies fared no better in their response, with one individual laughing nervously upon my mention of the film, only to realize that his uncontrolled, knee-jerk reaction was a faux pas on multiple levels. I do not draw from these moments any personal offense—though my instinctive desire to defend Yonfan's film and, by association, my project, may betray the permeation of this anxiety into my own consciousness. The film's queer soft-core subject matter—transgender prostitution in Singapore—and its campy, over-the-top, exploitation-style aesthetic approach do tempt many to respond in the manner I have described, justifiably or not. Such nervous responses, thus, demonstrate what Marjorie Garber argues in her book *Vested Interests: Cross-Dressing and Cultural Anxiety*, "that *transvestism is a space of possibility structuring and confounding culture*: the disruptive element that intervenes, not just a category crisis of male and female, but the crisis of category itself" (Garber 1992, 17, original emphasis).[1] Transgender politics' interventional possibilities on the questions of gender and sexuality can generate, rather fruitfully, discomfort and unease.

However, this anxiety does not simply rest on the level of responses to the film alone; it is also an extension of the cultural political anxiety surrounding the historical Bugis Street, a small geographical space near the business/commercial district in the island-nation of Singapore that has received much Western media attention in the past, much to the nationalist displeasure of some Singapore citizens. Queer activist Alex Au's diatribe, in his renowned *Yawning Bread* website, against the allusion to Bugis Street in a

---

1. Transgenderism and transvestitism are distinctive but overlapping concepts that I am not trying to conflate here. Instead, my goal is to draw upon the theoretical lesson offered by Garber that is applicable to transgender politics in general.

Scottish newspaper article about Singapore may be representative, if not symptomatic, of the irritations that Singaporeans frequently experience when Bugis Street headlines as a foreign obsession:

> Bugis Street again! Oh lord, won't they ever get off it? I'm old enough to have seen the real streetwalkers, and I can tell you, the transvestites were mostly past their use-by date. In any case, they were shoo'ed away from the area some 25 years ago, in the mid 70's.
>
> To Singaporeans today, Bugis Street means nothing. It certainly doesn't represent any golden age of excitement. It's a hand-me-down memory from lecherous, army grunts on R&R from the Vietnam War, too pissed-drunk even to stumble out of the brothels.
>
> Yet, a generation on, much writing about Singapore still sucks blood out of the Bugis Street reference. It's like a leech forever stuck on a bum, with a view of Singapore grotesquely limited by its fleshy contours. (Au 2002)

Au is correct to identify the nostalgic romantic glow that has enveloped the historical Bugis Street by means of the Orientalist gaze of Western tourists and travelers passing through Singapore's fair shores. He is also probably right, though hyperbolically, in his assertion that this fixation on Bugis Street (because of the sexual tourism it offered) is contrary to the contemporary Singaporean's dismissal of its cultural or historical importance—that "Bugis Street means nothing." What I take away from Au's resistance to the Western obsession with the historical Bugis Street, and the general reaction I received about my project on Yonfan's film, is less a disagreement on my part with their often understandable reaction to the problematic cultural discourses about this geographical space, but more a fascination with the unease, the anxious desire for cultural and historical amnesia, framed by the politics of nationalism, postcoloniality, and queer sexuality. It is an anxiety that conjures the contradictory specter of not just a messy and unsanitary age gone by, but also the troubling cultural politics that disturb Singapore's slick and squeaky clean image as a multicultural global city for the transnational capitalist set to work and play in. Since undertaking this in-depth analysis of Yonfan's film (and by extension the historical Bugis Street) makes me complicit in becoming one of those who "sucks blood out of the Bugis Street reference," I embrace this (and my own) anxiety with abandonment, to unpack the political, cultural, and cinematic discourses surrounding and inhabiting this space that is Bugis Street. This book, hence, is my small way of confronting and exorcizing the fraught relations that I (and other Singaporeans) have toward the ideological and material contradictions in the country's national cultural politics, as embodied in this seemingly slight "Bugis Street reference."[2] But on a more ambitious theoretical front, this book of specific filmic and cultural criticism offers a localized case study that inserts itself, I hope productively, into the scholarly conversations about the complications of postcolonial and queer sexual politics within the analysis of transnational Chinese and Asian cinemas. Thus, the central objective of this book is to demonstrate how Yonfan's *Bugis Street*, as a minor transnational text of cinematic

2. Even today, Bugis Street never quite disappears from Singapore's cultural landscape. In his online cataloging of things Bugis Street in the *Singapore LGBT Encyclopedia*, Roy Tan lists a photography exhibition and a series of public talks in Singapore in 2014 by Alain Soldeville. Titled "Bugis Street," the exhibition featured photographs of transgendered women that were, as Soldeville points out, "portraits of these people I had come to consider friends, wishing to show their fragility, their humanity rather than document-ing a situation, news style." The photos were taken in the early 1980s before the state closed down the space. Some of the photos are available at http://www.soldeville.com/data/pages/eng/bugisstreet.htm, accessed on January 23, 2015. Tan also reports that there is a second television season of a doc-umentary-drama in the works for MediaCorp's Channel 5, which features a segment on Bugis Street (Tan, "Bugis Street: Transgender Aspects").

intervention, offers a playful and fantastical representation of this small street in historical Singapore, not just to expose the cultural anxiety surrounding it, but also to engage the manifold issues of queer sexuality and politics as a means of deconstructing and critiquing the homophobic/transphobic institutional, legal, social, and cultural discourses that permeate postcolonial Singapore. Of course, such an analytical hermeneutic does not intend to celebrate unreflectively Yonfan's film as a politically utopian text, but instead it seeks to identify both its possibilities and its flaws, so as to begin to ask the difficult questions of transnational queer cinema (albeit only through a singular case study), of both its progressive political potentialities and its countervailing neoliberal complicities.

In the remainder of this extended introduction, I inscribe the contextual contours, in which to locate my later readings of the film, by (1) conducting a brief survey of Singapore history in terms of the geographical Bugis Street; (2) focusing on Yonfan's career and place in Hong Kong art-house and transnational cinema; (3) examining why *Bugis Street* as transnational cinema is a productive critical approach; and (4) providing a quick synopsis of the film's plot. Expanding upon these contextual parameters of Bugis Street as a cultural phenomenon, Chapter 1 explores a range of textual genres from a pop cultural archive I have gathered, in order to map out the key political discourses that have also populated the film. Chapter 2 extends the contextual framework to sexuality on Hong Kong and Singapore screens, focusing particularly on transgender prostitution and transgender representations, while also keeping in mind the politics of queer sexuality in these two different locales. Turning finally to filmic representation, I foreground in Chapter 3 the queer politics of *Bugis Street*, by taking on specifically the multifold sexual visualities that the film generates as forms of political intervention. Chapter 4 continues the queer critical analysis with a study of queer space and time as manifested in the film and how they inform a queer ethics of relationality. Concluding the book is a short chapter reflecting upon the politics of community that the analysis of *Bugis Street* has inspired.

Singapore's Historical Bugis Street

The notorious Bugis Street of yore has been relegated to the dust heap of Singapore's recent historical past, and maybe rightfully so, especially for those who consider it a relic of Orientalist sensationalism (like Alex Au of *Yawning Bread*) or for the older conservative majority who see this rather small space in downtown Singapore as a stain on Singapore's official narrative of neoliberal "progress" toward becoming a world-class global city and nation-state, with its squeaky clean image and reputation. If one were to ask today's younger generation about the old Bugis Street, one would be greeted by bafflement or an indifferent shrug. "Bugis" as a contemporary geographical marker is now associated with a station in the ultra-modern subway train system of the Singapore Mass Rapid Transit (SMRT). Exiting the station leads one into a series of crowded air-conditioned malls (Figure 1), including the appropriately named Bugis Junction (Figure 2). Across the street is an open-air street mall (Figure 3), the New Bugis Street, which is supposed to mimic the bustling atmospherics of the old Bugis Street. Any knowledge of its predecessor is probably culled from talk-stories passed down from the previous generation, who have lived through Bugis Street's heyday in the 1960s and 1970s; or from access to a pop cultural and literary archive that has reimagined that space into what Rey Chow might call "sentimental fabulations" (Chow 2007), thus filling the public discursive imagination with a version of Bugis Street as a signifier of both national alterity and unspoken desire. In Chapter 1, I will comb through aspects of this archive, to which the film *Bugis Street* obviously belongs, in order to unravel the ideological construction of this mythical-historical

Figure 1   Malls around the Bugis Street area (May 18, 2011), photo by author

Figure 2   Bugis Junction (May 18, 2011), photo by author

Figure 3   The New Bugis Street as open-air mall (May 18, 2011), photo by author

street and the discursive signals it emits about the culture and politics of contemporary Singapore. But, for now, I gather together some scattered historical notes about Bugis Street to, on the one hand, perform the requisite historical contextualization that any interpretation of such an archive conventionally demands; and to, on the other hand, suggest that this historical "facticity" is part and parcel of the cultural political narration and fabulation that go into the (inter)national fantasy that is Bugis Street.

Bugis Street was named after a Malay subgroup that inhabited the Malay and Indonesian archipelago.[3] One historian points out

3. The Chinese also called the area "Baishafu" (白沙浮), which is translated as "white sand mounds." During the Japanese occupation of the Second World War, "Black Street" was also another name used to describe the Japanese clubs present along the street. A 2006 MediaCorp Channel 8 documentary features aspects of this history. Part of this Singapore television program is

that at "the turn of the twentieth century, there were some 35,000 people living in Singapore who were classified as Malays, but within that group, there were ten subgroups, including the Bugis, Acehnese, Minangkabau, Javanese, Boyanese, Bidayuh, peninsular Malays, Madurese, Orang Laut and Arabs." Hence, "Singapore was the Malay melting pot of the archipelago" (Baker 2008, 106). However, as the grand dame of Singapore history Constance Mary Turnbull recounts, the history of the Bugis presence in Singapore runs all the way back to the early decades of the nineteenth century during the time of the first British Resident Colonel William Farquhar and the founder of British colonial Singapore Sir Stamford Raffles. The Bugis were traders who were caught in the Dutch-British rivalry of the region. When a group of 500 decided to settle in Singapore in 1820, Resident Farquhar allowed them to construct "their kampong on the Rochore River," believing that this "community of families . . . would attract the prized Bugis trade." The island "soon became the headquarters of Bugis trade in the western archipelago" (Turnbull 2009, 33–34). Raffles was more wary of the Bugis because of their involvement in the slave trade, which Raffles found repugnant, thus leading him to ban slavery in 1823 (41). He also transplanted the Bugis "further east [of the city center] beyond Kampong Glam," as part of his redistricting plans (38). By 1826, "[m]ost Indonesian and Arab immigrants settled in parts of the town still bearing their names, such as Kampong Jawa, Kampong Sumbawa, Bugis Street, and Arab Street" (68).

It is difficult to attribute Bugis Street's later salacious reputation to the ethnic community that once lived there, beyond the fact that the Bugis lent their namesake to the street.[4] However, one could

now available on YouTube entitled "History of Bugis Street" (Tan, "Bugis Street: Transgender Aspects").

4. The following coincidental ethnological resonance is worth noting, especially in terms of contemporary theories of gender and sexuality: according to anthropologist Susan Millar's fieldwork among the Bugis in Indonesia, "a

potentially argue that the area's peripheral proximity to the main commercial district offered a convenient corollary space for the growth of prostitution that quietly catered to the respectable set of British imperialism and Singapore's capitalist elite. Historically, demographics had a central role to play in this social phenomenon, as there was one female to eight males in the gender distribution in 1911, according to the census at the time (Turnbull 2009, 110). Especially in the Chinese community, "[p]rohibition would have been unrealistic in Singapore, where in 1884 there were 60,000 Chinese men but only 6,600 Chinese women, of whom [William] Pickering estimated that at least 2,000 were prostitutes. A ban would also have encouraged homosexual prostitution, which was supplied for many years by the importation of Hainanese boys" (101). This is not to say that the British colonial government did not try. While prostitution was left outside of its legislative net, the authorities managed to shut down brothels in 1930 (150). What is fascinating to me, though, is that the British, like the Americans during the Vietnam War, were not above moral complicity in the complex intertwining of sexuality, racial imperialism, and military might. Japanese reporter Tatsuki Fujii offered in 1938 a depiction

---

third gender category, composed of male transvestites called *calabai*," exists, thus supporting her thesis of the "nonbiological, or strictly social, Bugis conception of gender." These transvestites have historically "played important roles in the kingdoms as ritual specialists called *bissu*" and, now, also function "as curers or ritual specialists at weddings and other life-crisis events" (Millar 1983, 488). In a more recent study of "gender transgression" in Indonesia, Evelyn Blackwood points to the androgyny of divine entities inhabiting the Bugis religious universe, and where the *bissu* are their offspring (Blackwood 2005, 857). For a more detailed study of the various Bugis gender identities, see Davies (2007). Roy Tan speculates that "it is possible that transgender Singaporeans with a knowledge of this aspect of Bugis society first decided to congregate there in the 1950s because of this association" (Tan, "Bugis Street: Transgender Aspects").

of the sexual dalliances of British men: "For the younger bachelors, life in Singapore was very convenient. They usually started drinking at the Cricket Club, proceeded on to one of the three cabarets where they danced with a pretty Chinese or Eurasian partner and ended up at the cafes which lined Jalan Besar Road and Lavender Street. If the favors of certain dancers at the cabarets were unobtainable, they went along to one of the numerous brothels which served just as well" (Fujii 1994, 241–42). The streets referenced are found in the same geographical area where Bugis Street lies. If Fujii's representation is considered too jaundiced for some on account of Japan's aggression during the Pacific war, one can also turn to British travel author Carveth Wells's equally colorful 1939 description of the area:

> "*Pergi Malay Street!*" (Go to Malay Street) used to be the usual order to the ricksha [*sic*] puller after dinner in Singapore. This street used to be the heart of the segregated area of the city, where street after street was devoted entirely to brothels of different nationalities. Malays, Indians, Africans, Arabs, Chinese, Japanese and Europeans were all on view in all their war paint . . . Malay Street and the whole of Singapore's segregated area has been cleaned up and is now a respectable part of the city. (Wells 1994, 248)

Wells is obviously not quite accurate about the socio-moral cleansing, as much of the area has been restored to "respectability" only in the 1980s by a post-independence Singapore government.

In fact, Bugis Street gained its notoriety specifically in the 1950s as a spot for transgender prostitution, according to Koh Buck Song, literary author and, at a time, journalist for Singapore's main newspaper the *Straits Times*:

> A relatively short lane (about 130 metres long and 8 metres wide), Bugis Street is traversed by the junctions of Malabar

and Hylam Streets, and bounded by Victoria Street and North Bridge Road . . . British, Australian and other servicemen began frequenting the area for the cheap hawker fare in the late '40s and early '50s . . . It was around this time that the transvestites came on the scene and made their presence felt . . . The transvestite prostitutes came from the neighbouring areas . . . [and] were present from about 10pm to 5am. Most of them would appear after midnight, dressed in the women's apparel of the day, such as the Malay *sarong kabaya*, Indian *sari*, Chinese cheongsam and the most common, Western frocks. (Koh 1994, 158–59)[5]

In a series of newspaper articles that appeared in the tabloid-style *New Nation* in 1972, investigating homosexuality in Singapore,[6] national attention was brought to Bugis Street and the prostitution that was occurring there. The first article notes how "[t]he transvestites who have become prostitutes frequent Bugis Street . . . and Johore Road, in foul-smelling, oppressive hovels, honeycombed with box-like cubicles big enough only for a double bed and standing space for one or two." For rates at "$3 to $20 or more," they offered their services, "often fleecing European tourists or resident expatriates." The article observes how local customers congregated along Johore Road, while Bugis Street tended to focus on foreigners (Yeo, Khoo, and Lee 1972, 9).

5. Koh included a non-fiction section at the end of his *Bugis Street: The Novel* entitled "Bugis Street—A History," from which this quotation is extracted.

6. Touted as the first news focus on the taboo subject, this series of four articles (with a fifth featuring responses from the community) tried to cover a range of perspectives and featured interviews with quite a few queer Singaporeans. The articles devoted a substantial (if not inordinate) amount of space to Bugis Street and its transgender denizens—proving Bugis Street to be what Russell Heng has identified as "the first known instance of homosexuality finding expression as a local idiom" (Heng 2001, 82). These articles are available online, thanks to the untiring efforts of Roy Tan and Jun Zubillaga-Pow: http://sporelgbtpedia.shoutwiki.com/wiki/Singapore%27s_first_newspaper_articles_on_the_LGBT_community, accessed January 23, 2015.

The outsized reputation of this "relatively short lane" (Koh 1994, 158) grew to the point that even the British government, in a moment of homosexual panic, had the Royal Navy enact "a secret crackdown on gay sailors and officers in the late 1960s" (Travis 2002). This secret was only revealed in a report by *The Guardian* as late as 2002, a report that also demonstrated "that the 1969 panic over homosexuality in the navy was sparked . . . by concerns over the number of sailors ending up with the catamites of Bugis Street when on shore leave in Singapore" (Travis 2002). (I will return to this notion of homosexual panic in Chapter 1.) There was also an American presence during the period of the Vietnam War, where the newly independent Singapore was, and remains, a significant ally of the United States. Singapore was useful "as a supplies centre" and a port for ship repairs (Turnbull 2009, 304). Troops from Australia did not leave until 1973, with the British following suit in 1976 (312).

Figure 4 Bugis Street (1962). Courtesy of the National Archives of Singapore.

The enactment of the Land Acquisition Act of 1966 "gave the authorities a free hand in urban clearance and renewal . . . The population was dispersed from the crowded central areas where it had hitherto been concentrated" (Turnbull 2009, 317). Later urban renewal and the redeployment of the population to brand new government-built housing development estates in various parts of the island completely transformed the area of Bugis Street, thereby dispersing the transgender prostitution activity. According to one local news report, Bugis Street was shut down in 1986 so that an MRT station could be built (Kwan 1992). Ironically, the cleaning up of the spaces around the commercial district had a negative effect on tourism, as the Singapore government began to realize that "[t]he new towns and clean public housing . . . held little appeal for the tourist, who missed the picturesque spectacle of other people's poverty" (Turnbull 2009, 318). What Turnbull has so wittily and incisively identified in the touristic gaze and the government's catering to that gaze is a process of self-Orientalism that, to a certain degree, motivated the practices of cultural and heritage conservation in modern Singapore: "In 1986 the Urban Redevelopment Authority designed six conservation zones to restore the exotic East image of the old Chinatown, Kampong Glam, and Little India and to preserve part of Singapore's colonial heritage. Even the notorious transvestite haunt Bugis Street was rebuilt" (318). But, as Koh Buck Song observes, "the old nightspot . . . was not to be the same again." The authorities tried to simulate, in a Disney style, a sanitized version of the street culture by having transsexuals assume the role of "customer relations officers," a ploy that did not go down well, "following complaints from conservative quarters" (Koh 1994, 161), an ideologically and culturally straitlaced populace that, ironically, the state has very effectively cultivated for its own political gain. These expressions of self-righteous moral outrage were lodged against the new

Bugis Street despite assurances from the management that "[t]he customer relations officers were not allowed to solicit or leave the premises with customers" (Kwan 1992). In fact, a spokesperson for the company even noted how these transgender employees "are watched by closed-circuit TV cameras and plainsclothesmen [*sic*] and their services will [be] terminated if they do so" (quoted in Kwan 1992). The paranoiac panopticon of corporate surveillance is thus represented as a conscientious act of public service to protect Singapore citizens from, and to contain, the aberrant sexualities and gender identities that these transsexual customer relations officers represent. However, it also betrays Singapore's deep-seated cultural anxiety about Bugis Street, with which I began the introduction. As Maggie, one of the four customer relations officers (and who was a former Bugis Street sex worker and who also had a substantial role in Yonfan's film),[7] reminisces, "[i]n the old Bugis Street we were very free. The minute we got off our taxis at 10pm, we would fly like birds to our customers. Here we can only sit down at a table if someone calls us" (quoted in Kwan 1992). Her nostalgia for the old Bugis Street and the real material trace that she offers to that now absent social space provide the much-needed critical counterpoint to this cultural anxiety.

---

7. The transition of Maggie from the original Bugis Street, to the new Bugis Street, and finally to the filmic *Bugis Street* registers a real-to-reel conti-guity that ruptures the political, cultural, and institutional desire to erase the abject—which Bugis Street physically and discursively embodies—from Singapore's collective consciousness. I had the good fortune and privilege to meet Maggie during a talk I gave at FilmGarde Cineplex in Singapore on June 29, 2013, organized by the Asian Film Archive. I wish to thank her for her generosity in sharing her past experiences with me and for the news-related material she provided.

Yonfan as Transnational Hong Kong Filmmaker

The new millennium is seeing a revival of Yonfan's career in the international film festival circuit. A retrospective of seven Yonfan films was held at the 16th Busan International Film Festival in 2011 (Chu 2011a) and another at the 2012 Moscow International Film Festival (Kozlov 2012). Yonfan chaired the jury of the 2011 Asian Film Awards (Coonan 2011) and the jury for the New Currents Award at Busan 2011 (THR Staff 2011). Earlier, he was also a judge for the American Film Institute in 2009 (Yonfan 2012, 106). According to reports, Fortissimo Films will handle the distribution of the newly remastered versions of Yonfan's thirteen films (Chu 2011a): *A Certain Romance* (1984), *The Story of Rose* (1985), *Immortal Story* (1986), *Double Fixation* (1987), *Last Romance* (1988), *Promising Miss Bowie* (1990), *In Between* (1994),[8] *Bugis Street* (1995), *Bishonen* (1998), *Peony Pavilion* (2001), the documentary *Breaking the Willow* (2003), *Color Blossoms* (2004), and *Prince of Tears* (2009). Of course, this is a great boon for audiences and researchers alike, especially since some of his earlier films are still unavailable on DVD, while others can only be purchased in localized markets in Hong Kong.[9] This anticipated expansion of filmic distribution internationally will help cement Yonfan's reputation as a significant cinematic voice in both Hong Kong and global cinema, especially ever since *Bishonen* first placed him on the international map when it won the best picture prize at the Milan International Lesbian and Gay Film Festival in 1999.

While Yonfan's artistic talent is indisputable, his critical reputation is much more checkered. Before finding his place in

8. *In Between* is a portmanteau film made up of three short films, one of which Yonfan directed. Hence, technically, Yonfan has only made twelve full-length feature films.

9. At the moment, a number of Yonfan's recent films are available for sale on DVD through his website (www.yonfan.com).

the Hong Kong photography[10] and film scenes, the young Yonfan
migrated from Hunan, China, where he was born, to spend time in
Hong Kong, Taiwan, and the West.[11] In his memoir *Intermission*,
he chronicles how his father uprooted the family to move from
Mainland China, to Hong Kong, to Taiwan, before returning to
Hong Kong again as Yonfan turned sixteen (Yonfan 2012, 22, 41).
In the late 1960s and early 1970s, Yonfan went to America and
Europe to study and travel (101). He even hitchhiked in France to
visit Cannes, leading him to appreciate how this seaside town "was
the best place to earn a reputation for art films" (83).[12] Like many
aspiring actors, he worked as an extra in Hollywood, appearing
in movies like Robert Altman's *M*A*S*H* (1970) and Tom Gries's
The Hawaiians (1970) (110, 121). His diasporic background and
his later worldwide travels, in a sense, have granted him license
to christen himself "a director of the world," one whose cinematic
influences include Douglas Sirk and Federico Fellini (Li 2010). The
Sirkian and Fellinian inspirations are not surprising, considering
how Yonfan's filmmaking career has similarly straddled both
commercial and artistic realms. His oeuvre from 1984 to 1994
consisted mainly of Hong Kong romances and melodramas, many
with an art-film twist. They were also vehicles for notable star turns
from Hong Kong and Taiwan luminaries such as Carol Cheng,
Jacky Cheung, Cherie Chung, and Sylvia Chang. Yonfan could also
pride himself for casting the then nascent talents of Maggie Cheung
and Chow Yun-fat in his second film *The Story of Rose*—this was
before Cheung became a Hong Kong superstar in Wong Kar-wai's
critically acclaimed films, and before Chow rose to superstardom

---

10. His photographic work is also accessible on his website at http://www.yonfan.
    com/works.html.

11. Some of these biographical details are taken from Yonfan's resume on the
    Internet Movie Database: http://www.imdb.com/name/nm0948523/
    resume, accessed December 13, 2012.

12. All quotations from Yonfan's memoir are based on my own translation.

a year later in John Woo's *A Better Tomorrow* (1986). Yonfan's
accomplishments have led one critic to crown him, retroactively,
"a star maker in the Asian film world," particularly in reference to
"Daniel Wu, who took his first acting role in Yonfan's *Bishonen* in
1998 after the director spotted him in a television commercial" (Chu
2011b)—Wu has since gone on to become a mega Hong Kong film
star, appearing in high-profile productions like *2000 AD* (2000),
Around the World in 80 Days (2004), *House of Fury* (2005),
Protégé (2007), and *Tai Chi Hero* (2012).

While Yonfan's directorial work from 1984 to 1994 clearly
coincided with what Hong Kong film scholar Stephen Teo calls "the
second wave," with films "from 1984 to 1990" by now renowned
directors such as Wong Kar-wai and Stanley Kwan (Teo 1997, 160),
these earlier films by Yonfan have generated much less attention
than those of his more well-known Hong Kong filmmaking
peers. One could speculate that the uneven quality and the more
mainstream nature of the films might have diverted (and continue to
deflect) critical attention away from them, especially in the context
of the international film festival circuits and English-language
critical circles. This trajectory of his earlier work was clearly not
lost on the director himself, as *Bugis Street* in 1995 appears to
mark a new phase in Yonfan's cinematic vision and sensibility. In
an interview, he characterizes his post-1995 work in cosmopolitan
and artistically Romantic terms: "I do not classify myself by region.
I do not like to involve myself in commercial markets. In this way, I
am freer to make films which have artistic merits" (Li 2010). *Bugis
Street*, hence, is pivotal in Yonfan's self-makeover from commercial
Hong Kong filmmaker to global art-house director, with *Bishonen*
completing the transformation with international critical success.
Bugis Street began Yonfan's "project" called "the trilogy of the
minors" (Yonfan 1995),[13] which eventually included *Bishonen* and

13. I am citing from the cover of Yonfan's "movie book" for *Bugis Street*. He

Peony Pavilion. In the context of Yonfan's cosmopolitan cinematic makeover, I will go so far as to classify the trilogy as an instance of transnational queer cinema. The politics and problematics of the "queer" in transnational queer cinema will be addressed in greater detail in Chapter 2. But for now, it is necessary to attend to, though in brief notational form, the potentialities of the "transnational" as a theoretical category as it relates to Yonfan's *Bugis Street* and his other films that follow.

Bugis Street as Transnational Cinema

In an essay in a recent collection that deals with the now highly popular notion of "Sinophone cinemas" (Yue and Khoo 2014), Sheldon Lu assesses the field of Chinese cinema studies through a historicized and theoretical mapping of "four critical paradigms": (1) the national cinema, (2) the transnational cinema, (3) the Chinese-language cinema, and (4) the Sinophone cinema (Lu 2014).[14] While my goal here is not to engage deeply with Lu's assessments of each of the categories, the theoretical pause I place on each of them is to acknowledge the epistemological and political possibilities of all of these categories, as a necessary route toward the transnational as a critically efficient, hermeneutical frame for *Bugis Street* in this book. Of course, I also do not wish to celebrate the transnational as an inherently "positive" political lens, but to explore instead the complex dialectical relationships it has with the other critical categories that Lu has identified, thereby exposing the contradictory cultural politics it embodies and emits.

---

included two other presumably nonexistent titles, *New Park* (1996) and *Silver Screen* (1997), which I can only surmise to be his initial plan for the tripartite filmic project. *Bishonen* and *Peony Pavilion* probably took their place in the final form of the trilogy.

14. Lu credits Song Hwee Lim for theoretically listing the first three critical categories. See Lim (2006, 2–7).

Citing the work of Yingjin Zhang (2004) and Chris Berry and Mary Farquhar (2006), Lu rightly argues that "the national will not simply disappear in the current climate of globalization . . . The national persists in the transnational and the global" (Lu 2014, 16). To put it another way, the tensions and the contradictions within the transnational are forged by the persistence of the national, and vice versa. While the work of many Hong Kong–based filmmakers are very multinational/transnational/global in terms of production, funding, distribution, exhibition, and consumption, they can also be national in their diegetic emphasis and cultural identification—and Yonfan's films are no exception. For instance, his queer trilogy is situated in three different national locales: Singapore (*Bugis Street*), Hong Kong (*Bishonen*), and Mainland China (*Peony Pavilion*). *Bugis Street* is particularly fascinating in relation to a national perspective, especially since it can be thought of as belonging to both the Hong Kong and Singapore national film canons. As the first film that signaled the independent-cinema approach that Yonfan had adopted, it is also one that diegetically steps outside of Hong Kong, despite the fact that the screenplay is written by Fruit Chan, who is now known for directing some important Hong Kong films such as *Made in Hong Kong* (1997), *Durian Durian* (2000), and *Hollywood Hong-Kong* (2001).[15] It is shot entirely in Singapore and fictionally depicts an actual historical street on the island nation. Scholars of Singapore film claim that it belongs to an emerging and rapidly growing corpus of contemporary Singapore cinema. According to Jan Uhde and Yvonne Ng Uhde, in their encyclopedic tome on Singapore cinematic history *Latent Images*, "Singapore's film revival began in 1991" (Uhde and Uhde 2010, 73),

---

15. See the synopsis of the rerelease of the film, now entitled *Bugis Street Redux*, on the Fortissimo Film website: http://www.fortissimo.nl/catalogue_ lineup_title.aspx?ProjectId=96d36b17-e12e-4eb0-a5ad-9725ed8cf126, accessed December 19, 2012.

which was followed by a thematic focus in the independent filmic scene on "the 'other' Singapore, hidden under the surface of the country's conspicuous wealth and economic success, away from the spic-and-span boulevards and ritzy shopping centres," of which *Bugis Street* is an exemplary instance (74). Uhde and Uhde took particular care to note that Margin Films, the film's distribution company in the United States, has pitched *Bugis Street* "as the first commercial, 'anti-blockbuster' movie from Singapore." They also identified Djinn, who is now an upcoming Singaporean director in his own right, as having helped Yonfan in this project (77).[16] Financially, *Bugis Street* is also a Singapore production in that it is listed (on the Internet Movie Database) as Jaytex Productions' only film title. The company was "run by the Singaporean brother-and-sister team, Godfrey and Katy Yew, who served as the film's executive producer and producer respectively. The Yews have since moved their business outside Singapore" (Uhde and Uhde 2010, 78). But it is important to observe that the national emplacement of *Bugis Street* needs to be qualified by the fact that it is considered a minor and marginal cinematic text in the narration of Singapore's contemporary cinema history. How much of this marginality is inflected by the cultural anxiety I discussed at the beginning of this chapter is a subject for speculation. Nonetheless, it is fascinating that this national marginality the film challenges and troubles through transnational channels. To account for its ability to shuttle easily between Hong Kong and Singapore, and to attract global attention because of its queer subject matter, the film requires a more expansive paradigm beyond the national to appreciate its cultural and political potentiality as an interventional text within the national context of Singapore.

---

16. Djinn went on to direct *Return to Pontianak* (2001)—which also featured the star of *Bugis Street*, Hiep Thi Le—and the critically acclaimed *Perth* (2004).

The "Chinese-language" and "Sinophone" critical models can next be addressed together here, as they both rest on a Sinitic linguistic premise. Sheldon Lu points to a 1998 book review, by Emilie Yueh-yu Yeh in *Jump Cut*, of the collection *New Chinese Cinemas: Forms, Identities, Politics* (Browne et al. 1994), postulating that this is probably the first English-language instance where the term "Chinese-language cinema" is used to articulate the notion of *huayu dianying* (華語電影). Yeh was following the lead of Taiwanese and Hong Kong critics' deployment of this concept to resist the nationalist inflections of "Chinese Cinema" (Lu 2014, 19). It was meant to be, as Yeh suggests, "an ad hoc term" that does "not privilege any one of the three cinemas" of Mainland China, Hong Kong, and Taiwan (quoted in Lu 2014, 19; Yeh 1998, 74). Lu concludes his historical chronology of this critical model with his and Yeh's "definitive anthology," *Chinese-Language Film: Historiography, Poetics, Politics* (Lu and Yeh 2005). He argues that the term has subsequently become "widely accepted and used in film scholarship" (Lu 2014, 19), no doubt to his and Yeh's contribution to the field. While I appreciate Lu and Yeh's earnest intention to critique the nationalist and cultural centrism through this linguistic strategy, I am less confident of its efficacy, especially in view of the trenchant criticism offered by Ien Ang of the essentialism that language discourses are capable of, even in minority circles throughout the Chinese diaspora.[17] In other words, can one not analyze films that are made in other languages but still have these films fall within the cultural confines of Chinese cinemas? On this particular question, I am indebted to Song Hwee Lim's astute reevaluation of the category of "Sinophone

---

17. See Ang's book *On Not Speaking Chinese* (2001). Being partly Peranakan myself, and with elementary Chinese-language skills, I find myself identifying with Ang in terms of what it means, for instance, to be relegated to the social, cultural, and institutional margins in Chinese-dominated Singapore.

cinemas." Vis-à-vis "Chinese-language films," the Sinophone is a much more complex and politically creative concept that pushes the linguistic premise further by articulating and promoting a minor or marginal positioning that disturbs the essentialism and centrism in discourses about Chinese culture or the Chinese nation. In her book *Visuality and Identity: Sinophone Articulations across the Pacific*, Shu-mei Shih conceptualizes the Sinophone in the following manner: "Sinophone articulations . . . contain an anticolonial intent against Chinese hegemony . . . The dominant language of the Sinophone may be standard Hanyu, but it can be implicated in a dynamic of linguistic power struggles. As a major language, standard Hanyu is the object against which various minor articulations are launched resulting in its destandardization, hybridization, fragmentation, or sometimes outright rejection" (Shih 2007, 30–31).[18] Still, the sticking point for Song Hwee Lim is the issue of language as the political tool of choice. "For what is the 'Sino' in the Sinophone?" Lim asks. "In Shih's construction, the Sinophone is defined 'not by the race or nationality of the speaker but by the languages one speaks,'[19] but isn't this lingua-centrism itself a form of essentialism that denies access to one's cultural production and cultural identity via a language that is presumably not one's own?" (Lim 2011, 38). What does the Sinophone mean for those who "have lost their knowledge of the Chinese language" and "yet somehow identify themselves as Chinese through cultural symbols, rituals and traditions" (38)? Lim further problematizes the Sinophone on the level of the sonic by contending that "[t]he insistence that the Sinophone must sound—however hybrid, impure or creolized—like a Sinitic language, implies that the Sinophone's

---

18. The constraints of space allow me only to pinpoint a very brief moment in Shih's highly complex theorization of the Sinophone in her book, a concept that has also evolved over time in her other publications, as Lu observes (Lu 2014, 20–22).

19. Lim quotes from Shih (2007, 185).

potentialities will invariably be constrained because it must remain univocal and Sino-centric" (Lim 2014, 72).

Obviously, one can comfortably nestle Yonfan's body of work within the critical rubrics of "Chinese-language films" and "Sinophone cinemas." In fact, Mirana M. Szeto insists "that the Sinophone perspective becomes even more important for Hong Kong culture exactly because it is gradually disappearing into an undifferentiated vision of a growing China" (Szeto 2014, 120). Being a part of the Chinese-language and Sinophone cinematic circuit, Yonfan has not been afraid to tackle the queer politics of the Hong Kong-Taiwan-China triangle, as evident in *Bishonen*, *Peony Pavilion*, *Color Blossoms*, and *Prince of Tears*. *Bugis Street* marks an important linguistic departure precisely because it is set in Singapore. While he could have chosen to shoot the film entirely in Mandarin—which some mainstream local filmmakers have done, in line with the Singapore government's Mandarin-language policy—Yonfan chose instead the more politically resistant route to include "Standard" English, Singlish,[20] Mandarin, and other Chinese dialects in the script. The main character Lian, played by Vietnamese-American newcomer Hiep Thi Le, speaks a supposedly Malaysian-inflected English, while many other characters speak Singlish with playful abandonment. The only significant character who uses Mandarin exclusively is Maggie, but her placement in the midst of the other supporting cast produces a rainbow coalition of multiculturalism that more accurately reflects the organic linguistic reality on the ground, as opposed to the state's artificially engineered, official four-language policy. (The Singapore government's economically pragmatist approach to culture has led to a linguistic and educational policy that promotes Standard English, Mandarin,

---

20. Singlish is an English patois that includes a hybrid smattering of Malay, Mandarin, and some Chinese dialects. Yonfan clearly chose to include it for localized linguistic authenticity.

Malay, and Tamil as the nation's official languages, at the expense of Singlish and the other Chinese dialects.) Mandarin is configured as only one of the multiple languages spoken in the film and is, thus, sonically and culturally deemphasized. Foregrounding Singlish and Chinese dialects, especially in the early 1990s in Singapore cinema, was considered a politically radical move. Such a tactic was similarly adopted by some Singapore filmmakers like Eric Khoo (at around the same time as *Bugis Street* in the 1990s), Colin Goh and Yen Yen Woo (in their 2002 film *Talking Cock the Movie*),[21] and, most recently, Royston Tan (especially in the use of Singlish and the Hokkien dialect in his first feature film *15* [2003] about juvenile gangsters). The point that Song Hwee Lim makes about Tan's *15* is particularly telling about the inadequacies of the Sinophone model, which one could also apply to *Bugis Street*:

> If the descendents [*sic*] of immigrants are to be expunged from the Sinophone community once they "no longer speak their ancestors' languages,"[22] given the hybridity of identities and the multiplicity and creolisation of languages of these peoples in their countries of residence, how does one judge at which point these languages are no longer spoken? (Lim 2011, 38)

15's intermingling of Singlish, Malay, Hokkien, and Mandarin renders its "dialogue . . . almost indecipherable to Chinese speakers outside of Singapore and Malaysia." Hence, "the qualification in Shih's Sinophone model assumes a certain level of linguistic purity whose boundary will be impossible to police" (38). Again, as in the case of "Chinese national cinemas," the "Chinese-language films" and the "Sinophone cinemas" are useful in engaging very specific points of cultural critique, though less useful than "transnational

---

21. For a detailed analysis of the film, see Groppe's essay "'Singlish' and the Sinophone" (Groppe 2014, 158–65).
22. Again, Lim quotes from Shih (2007, 185).

cinemas" in accounting for the border-crossing and interventional potential of *Bugis Street* as a cross-cultural film.

On the heels of Sheldon Lu's groundbreaking *Transnational Chinese Cinemas* (Lu 1997b) came much critical analysis in the field of Chinese cinemas, over the past two decades, that engaged the problematics of the transnational—I am thinking specifically of the work of Esther Yau (2001), Kwai-Cheung Lo (2005), Meaghan Morris, Siu Leung Li, and Stephen Chan Ching-kiu (2005), Gina Marchetti (2006), and my own book on the topic (Chan 2009), to name just a few—and, hence, it is not my desire to rehash here the key issues and concerns that transnational cinema raises. However, I want to offer two observations that do inflect my categorization of Yonfan's trilogy as "transnational queer cinema." Firstly, much of Hong Kong cinema (especially films leading up to and beyond the 1997 British handover of Hong Kong to the People's Republic of China), to be financially viable or successful, must consider its place in the global market and its ability to crisscross national and cultural boundaries, especially through the film festival network as a gateway to reach more mainstream international audience sectors. Hong Kong cinema could be considered as transnational through its reconfiguration of localized Hong Kong/Chinese culture for global consumption, another instance of the global/local dynamic at work. It is in this context that I have come to understand Yonfan's wish to "not classify . . . [himself] by region" and to envision himself as "a director of the world" (Li 2010), all of which feeding into the transnationality of his artistic production. Secondly, *Bugis Street* is also important as transnational cinema for a number of reasons. Its cast features Singaporean actors and the Vietnamese-American lead Hiep Thi Le, whose chief claim to fame is her role in Oliver Stone's *Heaven and Earth* (1993). Raphaël Millet makes this same point about the casting of Le by arguing that it helps "better position the movie in the international scene." He also notes that because the film "was shot in English, Mandarin and Cantonese," it allows itself to be marketed as "a regional product with potentially some international appeal" (Millet 2006, 102–3). The narrative of the film also takes on transgenderism, a hot topical commodity since the international triumph of Australian Stephan Elliott's *The Adventures of Priscilla, Queen of the Desert* (1994) and Hollywood's version of *To Wong Foo, Thanks for Everything! Julie Newmar* (1995).

These observations of mine are relatively mundane ones, considering the critical ubiquity of the transnational in Chinese cinema studies and the notion that "[t]ransnational cinema in the Chinese case as well as in the rest of the world is the result of the globalization of the mechanisms of film production, distribution, and consumption" (Lu 1997a, 3). The fait accompli of cinema as a transnational medium, hence, begs the question as to what is so significant about adopting the transnational as a critical mode for filmic analysis? The response that Chris Berry provides is that the proliferation of transnational capitalist networks and systems globally in the twentieth century has turned "the transnational . . . [into] a *world order* that . . . plays a role in shaping all Chinese filmmaking activities today . . . In these circumstances, the very widespread usage of the term in the last decade and more is completely understandable, and cannot be dismissed simply as fashion" (Berry 2011, 15; emphasis mine). While it is necessary to critique this new world order and its neoliberal underpinnings, Berry also argues that not "all film-makers operating in the space opened up by the transnational order are operating according to the principles of profit maximisation and accumulation" (13). In fact, as Sheldon Lu points out, "[t]he transnational is not necessarily an accomplice of triumphant transnational capitalism . . . One may speak of commercial transnational cinema, independent art-house transnational cinema, exilic transnational cinema and so forth"

(Lu 2014, 17). Ultimately, Berry's and Lu's conceptualizations of transnational cinema studies gesture toward what Will Higbee and Song Hwee Lim have termed as a "critical transnationalism," a theoretical model on which this book aspires to adopt. Their detailed description deserves to be quoted at length here:

> In the study of films, a critical transnationalism does not ghettoize transnational film-making in interstitial and marginal spaces but rather interrogates how these film-making activities negotiate with the national on all levels—from cultural policy to financial sources, from the multiculturalism of difference to how it reconfigures the nation's image of itself. In examining all forms of cross-border film-making activities, it is also always attentive to questions of postcoloniality, politics and power, and how these may, in turn, uncover new forms of neocolonialist practices in the guise of popular genres or auteurist aesthetics. It scrutinizes the tensions and dialogic relationship between national and transnational, rather than simply negating one in favour of the other . . . [I]t understands the potential for local, regional and diasporic film cultures to affect, subvert and transform national and transnational cinemas. It may also wish to pay attention to the largely neglected question of the audience and to examine the capacity of local, global and diasporic audiences to decode films as they circulate transnationally . . . constructing a variety of meanings ranging from adaptation and assimilation to more challenging or subversive readings of these transnational films. (Higbee and Lim 2010, 18)

It is my hope that the critical interpretations of *Bugis Street*, in this book, as border-crossing modes of queer intervention will ultimately be viewed as modest steps toward this project of a critical transnational cinema studies.

Synopsis of *Bugis Street*

In abiding by the practices of other books in this genre, I deem it necessary to provide a brief synopsis of the film under analytical consideration. Readers who are familiar with Yonfan's film can proceed directly to Chapter 1. Here is the basic plot: *Bugis Street* opens with the transgender prostitute Lola (Ernest Seah) picking up an American sailor (David Knight) along the eponymous street for sex. In the morning, the sailor angrily refuses to remunerate Lola for her services when he realizes that she is transgender. It is only when Lola solicits the aid of triad gangsters that the sailor finally relents and reluctantly pays her. His exit from Sin Sin Hotel coincides with the arrival of Lian (Hiep Thi Le), who has just traveled from Melaka, Malaysia, in order to work at the hotel as a wait-staff, domestic helper, and receptionist. Lian gets to know the hotel manager Mrs. Hwee (Gerald Chen) and the various prostitutes and transgender occupants living there, including Lola, Zsa Zsa (Mavia), Sophie (Sofia), Maggie (Maggie Lye), Dr. Toh (Matthew Foo), and Linda (Linden). One evening, as she enters Linda's room to deliver a bowl of noodles, Lian discovers to her horror that Linda is a man from her waist down. So traumatized is Lian that she almost leaves town, if not for Lola's advice to her to stay on at Sin Sin Hotel. As Lian settles into her new environment, she soon realizes that Lola's boyfriend Meng (Michael Lam) desires her. Compounding Lian's confusion with her sexual awakening is the arrival of Drago (Greg-O), a transgender salesperson from Paris. Drago bonds with Lian over the question of love and romance. She teaches Lian how to desire men, leading Lian to develop a crush on an anonymous schoolboy. One crazy evening during the arrival of sailors on their way to the Vietnam War, a party develops in the hotel. Zsa Zsa, Sophie, Lola, and Drago give Lian a makeover, dressing her up like a transgender prostitute. That evening, after a fight breaks out on Bugis Street, Lian runs back to the hotel only to encounter Meng again in Lola's room. Lian successfully rebuffs Meng's advances and develops a confident sense of female self because of the makeup and outfit that she has on. But Lian's confusion only deepens and turns into depression when Drago's mother (Lily Ong) dies in her hospital bed and Drago leaves Sin Sin Hotel. Man Kit (Sim Boon Peng), Lian's former employer's son, visits her from Melaka because he misses her. Lian, however, rejects his affections and asks him to return home. After seeing him off at the jetty, Lian encounters the schoolboy whom she has a crush on, only to find out that he does not even know of her existence. These setbacks lead Lian down the inevitable road of losing her virginity to Meng, who immediately abandons her after their sexual liaison. Completely overwhelmed by her troubles, Lian finally turns to Lola for solace. The latter's wisdom fortifies Lian and restores her *joie de vivre*.

1

Bugis Street as Pop Cultural Archive

Problematizing the Archive

My intention for this chapter is to continue the historical and cultural contextualization I have begun in the introduction by collating a popular cultural "archive" (of an online news article, a blog entry, poetry, colonial travel literature, a memoir, television documentaries, and a novel) about the historical Bugis Street and, hence, establishing the thematic contours that have enabled the production and cultural presence of Yonfan's *Bugis Street*. However, the linearity of this critical practice troubles me, though not enough to abandon the practice *in toto*, but sufficient to rethink the relationship between this archive—which I have somewhat randomly[1] assembled for analysis—and Yonfan's film, which has

---

1. My use of the phrase "somewhat randomly" denotes that this "archive" is composed of items that I have, indeed, randomly selected for their ideological significance, and items that have undisputedly found their way into the discursive idealization of Bugis Street within the public imagination, both

taken its place in this archive since 1995. This rethinking is meta-critically achieved through the ideas of Jacques Derrida and Rey Chow, which I will summarily link together into a theoretical instrument that I can then use to unpack these various "archival" texts and their ideological and cultural connections to the film.

In his book *Archive Fever*, based on a London lecture that he delivered in 1994, Jacques Derrida, in his quintessentially quixotic and brilliant fashion, revolutionizes the way we conceptualize archives and archival work by deconstructing the archival impulse and, thus, revealing its inherent contradictions. He exposes the intrusive productivity that is veiled by the archive's supposedly positivistic neutrality in the processes of gathering, labeling, and categorizing as part of its indexical functionality:

> [T]he archive, as printing, writing, prosthesis, or hypomnesic technique in general is not only the place for stocking and for conserving an archivable content *of the past* which would exist in any case, such as, without the archive, one still believes it was or will have been. No, the technical structure of the *archiving* archive also determines the structure of the *archivable* content even in its very coming into existence and in its relationship to the future. The archivization produces as much as it records the event. This is also our political experience of the so-called news media. (Derrida 1995, 16–17)

The archive is structured and structures itself in that "it records the event"—which in our case is the space and culture of Bugis Street—as much as it "produces" it: it memorializes it, relives it, (re) writes it, (re)imagines it, (re)interprets it, and even retroactively

---

Singaporean and global. Therefore, the collation and the analysis of this archive are in no way meant to be exhaustive in both scope and approach. For a more extensive and thorough online catalog, see Tan, "Bugis Street: Transgender Aspects".

fantasizes about it as a culturally and politically significant past, in order to reinsert it into our desires of and for the future. Like a temporal Mobius strip, the archival restructuring (of Bugis Street) engages what Derrida calls a "spectral messianicity" (36), a promising notion of futurity.

It is also important to think about this intrusive productivity as problematizing the conservational integrity of the archival project. According to Derrida, inherent in the archive is "a destruction drive, to contradict even the conservation drive, what we could call here the *archive drive*. It is what I called earlier, and in view of this internal contradiction, *archive fever*. There would indeed be no archive desire without the radical finitude, without the possibility of a forgetfulness which does not limit itself to repression" (19). To ask the question in another way: what constitutes the selective criteria for conservation, especially when what we leave behind in the dust heap of history is probably as significant as what we aestheticize to be deserving of narrative inclusion and cultural museumization? One can pose this question too about the archival truth behind the historical Bugis Street. Whether it is for those who romanticize Bugis Street with a glow of nostalgic fondness, or denounce it as the reputed space of excessive consumption, drunkenness, and debauchery, or for the majority of us who have little to no experience of this lost remnant of Singapore's past, its reconstruction through a popular cultural archive is particularly complex in terms of libidinal identifications, discursive emplacements, and political repressions. Bugis Street twists and turns in our historical, cultural, and political consciousness and imagination in ways unexpected. The various representational choices and registers that the texts (that I discuss in this chapter) make can, therefore, be both predictable and surprising. Conversely, they can also be repressive and destructive in their *prolific* expressions of what they conceive of as the horrors and degeneracies of Bugis Street.

I am also semantically and theoretically generous in my use of the term "archive" here, vis-à-vis the more disciplinarily stringent usage in the social sciences as privileging archivable items that signify or suggest historical facticity instead of literary and artistic fictions. In other words, I am less critically interested in an archive that is driven by the epistemological goal of distinguishing the "real" from the "fake" (which is not to suggest that I am not concerned about what the historical Bugis Street was like, or that such a project is of no cultural importance to the writing of Singapore history). Rather, in leaving the cultural anthropological work of divining the historical Bugis Street in the more capable hands of historians, my project here is more transfixed by the ideological drives behind the various modes of representation to which Bugis Street has been subjected. An assumption behind the hermeneutical work of this book is that the task of the historian is further complicated by the intermingling flows between fact and fiction, as the lines between the two blur in public discourses about Bugis Street. My goal, therefore, is to map these discursive flows in the pop cultural archive that has been assembled, and then to situate my readings of the film *Bugis Street* amidst these flows.[2]

Finally, it is in the context of fact-fiction meshing that I want to suggest the appropriated concept of "fabulation" for deployment here. In British author Julian Barnes's satirical and fictional enactment of historical writing, *A History of the World in 10½ Chapters*, a delusional character engages in what her therapist describes as "fabulation," where "[y]ou make up a story to cover the facts you don't know or can't accept. You keep a few true facts

---

2. To be true to the deconstructive fervor of the Derridean approach to the archive, I painfully acknowledge my own ideological hand in repopulating this Bugis Street archive by having discursively gathered these texts together in this chapter. I can only hope that readers will pardon my complicity on the grounds of my intended critique of the ideological forces that generated these archivable items in the first place.

and spin a new story round them. Particularly in cases of double stress" (Barnes 1989, 109). Barnes expands the concept beyond the character's delusional mechanism of psychological coping to rethink History, or histories, as a mode of national, cultural, and ideological coping. This notion of "fabulation" is thus turned inside out to assume a "positive" modality or inflection, not unlike the way Maxine Hong Kingston appreciates the instrumentality of talk-stories in her memoir, where it is difficult to "separate what is peculiar to childhood, to poverty, insanities, one family, your mother who marked your growing with stories, from what is Chinese? What is Chinese tradition and what is the movies?" (Kingston 1976, 5–6). This idea of fabulation as a flexible political aesthetic Rey Chow also arrives at philosophically through Friedrich Nietzsche and Gilles Deleuze, but she coaxes out of the term a productive nuance by attaching the sentimental adjectivally. "Sentimental fabulations," hence, is not just a subset of fabulations, but sentimentality frequently characterizes the motivations for and the tone of fabulations. Sentimentality draws feelings out of the archive that the sterile objectivity of historical facticity does not adequately do. "[T]he sentimental," according to Chow, "instead of being equated with the occurrence of affective excess per se, can more fruitfully be rethought as a discursive constellation—one that traverses affect, time, identity, and social mores, and whose contours tend to shift and morph under different cultural circumstances and likely with different genres, forms, and media" (Chow 2007, 17). While Chow does not disavow the theoretical necessity of "exposing . . . [sentimentalism's] ideology-ridden assumptions," her book's analysis of sentimental fabulations in a select list of contemporary Chinese films forces one "to think through the fantasy structures of accommodation and endurance that develop and multiply around such extravagances and strategies: the economic and moral forms of submission and subjectivization they solicit, the imaginary resolutions they supply to social antagonisms, and, most important, the formal and cognitive ruptures within them that, however tangentially or even unnoticeably, signal possibilities for perversion, subversion, and diversion" (22). My hope is to arrive at similar conclusions but with more localized inflections in my subsequent analyses of the Bugis Street archive and Yonfan's film.

The remainder of this chapter will take readers into the Bugis Street archive through five specific thematic contact points—(1) homosexual panic, (2) the allure of Asian alterity, (3) nostalgia and queer liberal politics, (4) Bugis Street reconstructed, and (5) Bugis Street reclaimed—with each thematic section focusing on an archival text of a different genre, as specific deconstructive case studies. Each thematic point is, of course, not just restricted to the specific text or the genre in each case; the themes discursively overlap and/or intersect one another, especially when it comes to *Bugis Street* the film.

Homosexual Panic

In the case involving Bugis Street and the British Royal Navy, which I briefly referenced in the introduction, the British newspaper *The Guardian* in 2002 offered an exposé article about government files dating back to 1969 detailing "a secret crackdown on gay sailors and officers." Because "homosexuality was so rife throughout the fleet," the authorities could only be selective in their disciplinary actions. There were "concerns over the number of sailors ending up with the catamites of Bugis Street when on shore leave in Singapore." The author of the news article is on the mark in describing this institutionalized melodrama as a "panic over homosexuality in the navy" (Travis 2002).

The triangulated relationship between imperialism, hetero-sexual masculine relations, and homosexual panic defines the homophobic anxieties and disciplinary structures in Euro-American cultures, as Eve Kosofsky Sedgwick argues in her books *Between Men* (Sedgwick 1985) and *Epistemology of the Closet* (Sedgwick 1990). She observes how "'homosexual panic' is the most private, psychologized form in which many twentieth-century western men experience their vulnerability to the social pressure of homophobic blackmail" (Sedgwick 1985, 89). The privileging of homosocial connections that gird Western male relationships places men in a "double bind," leading to "the acute *manipulability*, through the fear of one's own 'homosexuality,' of acculturated men; and . . . [to] a reservoir of potential for *violence* caused by the self-ignorance that this regime constitutively enforces. The historical emphasis on enforcement of homophobic rules in the armed services in . . . England and the United States supports this analysis" (Sedgwick 1990, 186).

Sedgwick's reference to the military and its masculinist culture, as they exemplify homophobic oppression and anxiety, is not coincidental, for obvious reasons. But what is intriguing in this specific case involving Singapore's Bugis Street and its entanglement with the remnants of British imperial presence in this freshly independent postcolonial nation is that the gendered signification in the figure of the hetero-masculinized British soldier, with stiff upper lip and aloof propriety, has been subverted. To be beguiled by the authentically feminine calls of sirens in a faraway exotic land is one thing; but to be ensnared by these transgender monsters into their hellish lair that was Bugis Street is another. This homosexual panic took on an almost comical, if it were not so offensive, caricature:

> Service chiefs agonised over the practice of sailors visiting the catamites of Bugis Street. The file says many sailors visited the area "for kicks," got drunk and "end up sleeping with male prostitutes known as catamites" who dressed up convincingly as females.

Captain MacIntyre reports that some of them were beautiful, dressed well and smelled delicious. "Many senior staff have visited Bugis Street to see for themselves and agree that they also could easily be fooled ONCE."

The admiralty decided to give all crews visiting Singapore a stern vice squad lecture on the grounds that the young sailors were not hardened homosexuals. (Travis 2002)

The military reports attempt to salvage the heterosexual masculinity of the navy by assuring its readers that its men "were not hardened homosexuals," as the drunkenness and the frivolity of Bugis Street had temporarily impaired their otherwise regimented and disciplined good judgment. It seems gratuitous for Captain MacIntyre to even suggest that there was a need for his senior military staffers to authenticate the gender trickery of the prostitutes, in order that he might find their feminine mimicry, if I may borrow Homi K. Bhabha's phraseology from a different context, "almost the same, but not quite" (Bhabha 1994, 86). The emphatic "ONCE" secures the heteronormative and absolves the young sailors of their momentary indiscretion by attributing it to inebriated misrecognition.

But what is critically delectable here is this slippery obscure object we call desire, which slips and slides between the cracks and interstices of official discourse. For a senior officer to bespeak of *transgender* visual beauty and olfactory delight is to betray the manner with which homoerotic desire permeates the spectrum of homosocial relations, deconstructing the panicky insistence on the homosexual-heterosexual binary opposition. The fact that this article also reveals how Bugis Street has crept into the eroticized radar of the military, the British government, and British public discourse exposes an unspoken and, often, unacknowledged queer libidinal gaze upon an exotic, queer Asian Other, as so effectively emblematized by the apparently delusional character Rene

Gallimard in David Henry Hwang's play *M. Butterfly* (Hwang 1988), whose queerness is disavowed despite its material necessity for his sexual liaison with Song Liling to be possible, a relationship that spans almost thirty years.

My critique of homosexual panic by the British Royal Navy over Bugis Street is not intended to be solely anticolonial in its inflection; for this homophobic anxiety is also resplendently evident in postcolonial Singapore's compulsory military service as part of the country's larger project of nation-building. Service men, upon enlistment, are ideologically interpellated into the discourse of nationalist heterosexual manhood—the idea that the military's role is to turn boys into men—though this process is similarly not as smooth or seamless as it is not so in the case of the British navy.[3] The nodes of contact between heteronormativity, militarism, and nationalism demarcate a national political constellation into which a non-sexualized Bugis Street is situated, and where a queer sexualized Bugis Street of the past is dissolved (or reconfigured) for the greater ideological good of the nation.

"Call of the East": The Allure of Asian Alterity

What is implicit in the British Royal Navy's homosexual panic, of course, is not just with the idea of sexual entanglements with its (former) colonized feminized Other, but is more so with regard to the

3. See Chris K. K. Tan's essay for a complex examination of homosexuality and military service in Singapore (Tan 2012). My personal experience in the Singapore Armed Forces has also opened my eyes to the tactical embedding of queer sexualities—which Tan's essay analyzes—that simultaneously circumvents and reifies the logic of a national compulsory heterosexuality. This complexity is cinematically depicted in Ong Keng Sen's *Army Daze* (1996) and tangentially, though not insignificantly, in Ekachai Uekrongtham's *Pleasure Factory* (2007). I have briefly discussed these Singaporean films elsewhere (Chan 2012, 168–69).

queerness of these entanglements. While heterosexual colonizer-colonized relations were probably not encouraged, the sexual allure of the East was a given and the sailors' sexual exploits in a foreign land were tolerated. In fact, this allure is a sexual extension of the grander discourse of Oriental mystique, a patriarchal, sexist, and racist reimagining of Asia to justify European colonial presence in this part of the globe in the nineteenth and twentieth centuries. Or, as the late Edward Said has put it more than three decades ago, Orientalist discourse is "a Western style for dominating, restructuring, and having authority over the Orient" (Said 1978, 3). In furthering his point about the relationship between artistic/literary culture and the project of Western imperialism—in *Orientalism*'s follow-up book, *Culture and Imperialism*—Said argues that "stories are at the heart of what explorers and novelists say about strange regions of the world" (Said 1993, xii) and that "the challenge is to connect" culture to "the imperial process of which they were manifestly and unconcealedly a part" (xiv). However marginal it may be, Bugis Street has been inscribed into British imperialism's cultural epistemology. While it was institutionally endured and from which it was morally distanced, Bugis Street has also been ideologically embraced as part of the dangerous allure of the mystical East. The two cultural texts in which I have encountered interesting references or allusions to Bugis Street are a travel book by F. D. Ommanney entitled *Eastern Windows* (Ommanney 1962) and a book of poetry written by Barrington Kaye called *Bugis Street Blues* (Kaye 1955).

Like most entries in the genre of colonial travel literature, Ommanney's *Eastern Windows*, as the title not so subtly suggests, opens a window, and a tinted one at that, into the exotic East for the curious European reader. Hence, Ommanney predictably packs his book with colorful descriptions of the indigenous denizens that rival, though much poorly, Tolkien's depictions of the otherworldly characters in *The Lord of the Rings*.[4] Arriving in "Singapore as an officer in the Research branch of the Colonial Service" in 1952 (Ommanney 1962, 15), the author heeded what he construes as "the Call of the East," which he rather derogatorily describes as "that mysterious disease, which is still very real and catching and compelling." In the same breath, he signals the sexual charge in the air by pointing out that one "never can forget the beauty and grace of the people, their blue-black hair and the exquisite drawing of the oriental eye . . . Thighs and breasts and hips move with a gayer, lighter rhythm" (14). In another revelatory moment, he obsesses about the sensual physicality of touch between "Oriental" men:

> The streets were full of slight, wiry little men who walked holding up the corners of their skirts one in either hand, or looped them up around their waists above their skinny calves. Many of them walked in couples holding hands, their little fingers linked together. This is a universal oriental habit. You see men walking hand in hand among all the races of the Far East and Africa too . . . It is a habit which gives a feeling of friendly propinquity and companionship. It has no other significance, such as might attach to it in the West. To orientals, who have not had a non-conformist movement, nor an Oscar Wilde case, nor read the more thunderous parts of the Bible, such an idea would never occur. (27)

---

4. Ommanney conjures up the following image of, probably, an Indian vagrant, when he stepped off the ship onto Singapore shores for the very first time: "One of the figures crouching under a damp gunny sack in the shelter of the warehouse roof uncoiled itself and came to life. It was a small black gnome. It had a bald head and the whites of its eyes were yellow. Its lips and irregular teeth were red with betel juice. It had a barrel-shaped body in a dirty blue shirt and even dirtier blue and white striped shorts, below which a pair of thin, bird-like legs emerged, covered with what looked like fine black wire. This figure of salvation did a little dance before me, making a pantomime to imitate carrying a load on its shoulders. It pointed to itself, nodding its head, to indicate that it was suggesting itself as a porter" (Ommanney 1962, 25–26).

The sexual anxiety is palpable in his ludicrous suggestion that because gay sexuality has not been politicized in Asia at that particular time, it is, therefore, not possible for gay contact between Asian men to exist. (I am not saying that Ommanney is completely wrong in his observation of this Asian practice. Many can attest to seeing Indian men holding hands in Singapore, for instance, a practice that is often platonic in its signification. What I am problematizing here is the way Ommanney has deployed his understanding of Oriental "Culture" to foreclose, carte blanche, any other sexual possibilities.) The contradictory simultaneity of hetero-eroticism and queer erasure exposes the compensatory need to deal with any sexual uneasiness that the rupturing of the heterosexual-homosexual binarism compounds.

In the chapter on the Singapore "Street Scene," Ommanney devotes nine of the twelve pages (38–46) to Bugis Street, as he shifts in tone between an abstract condescension and a mildly altruistic concern for the prostitutes of the area. This was a time when most of the prostitutes in Bugis Street were female, with transgender prostitutes only beginning to make their presence felt, one of whom Ommanney presents to us in detail:

> And now here comes Maisie, tall and graceful too, but perhaps a trifle over-slim and flat-chested. She wears a smart, black, sheath-like *cheong-sam* with little jet beads sewn in patterns. They shimmer as she walks . . . But there is something not quite right about her feet. They are a shade too large. I will tell you a secret about Maisie. No one is supposed to know it, but it is surprising how many do. She is not a girl at all. She is a boy. Sometimes clients have been known to make quite a scene when they discover their mistake, and Maisie has sometimes had to stay away from Bugis Street for a day or two nursing a black eye. But not for long. Nothing daunted, she will be back again in a day or two with a new *cheong-sam* and some new ear-rings. (44)

Maisie is part of a menagerie of erotic figures that Ommanney has populated in his representation of Bugis Street. The eroticism is a necessary enticement that Western travel literature offers, which has consequently helped constitute the foundations of today's global sex tourism. Maisie is the transgender sexual flavor in the erotic and exotic range of prostitutes on offer in Ommanney's Bugis Street. This special privilege that Ommanney grants his readers here is a gaze through the window into the "secret" sexual mysteries of the Orient: that Maisie "is not a girl at all" but "is a boy," and that the inscrutability of the Orient can play sexual Russian roulette on a person, because what one sees may not be what one gets, a game that can be sexually enticing play for some. Maisie has also been carefully and suggestively read as a "boy" in order to retain the feminization of Asian males, a reading that further coincides with the supposed impossibility of gay relations between Asian men, which Ommanney has established earlier. This reading cracks open and leaves slightly ajar the door for queer tendencies of the colonial subject to step through, while keeping intact the heterosexual normalcy of Empire. Finally, Ommanney registers his sentimental attachment (as Rey Chow would put it) to Singapore by fixating on Bugis Street as a space where "everything is possible" and where "after midnight male egos in their hundreds drift there . . . Or you can just sit there, as I used to, and let time slide past like a dark river" (46). He closes the book with another reference to his beloved Bugis Street by acknowledging how simultaneously "beautiful and *louche*" (244) it was, a contradiction that emblematizes the fabulated place that the Asian Other occupies in the discourses of sexual anxiety plaguing the colonial subject.

The love-hate, desire-repulsion, dynamic that interlines colonial sentimentality with Bugis Street in *Eastern Windows* finds a different material iteration in the poetry of Barrington Kaye, though both appear to lead to similar conclusions about the Asian allure. Kaye has given his collection *Bugis Street Blues* the following subtitle: *A Sentimental Guide to Singapore*. While the affectation of poetry is what he probably has in mind in describing his work as "sentimental," I am wondering what sentimental attachments does he have to Singapore per se, especially from a sociological perspective? Kaye describes himself in his biographical profile, at the time of the publication of *Bugis Street Blues*, as "a Social Research Fellow of the University of Malaya," who is "trained as a sociologist at the London School of Economics" (Kaye 1955). In choosing the poetic mode as the means of articulating his feelings of attachment to Singapore, how does the sociological scholarly detachment from the object of study dovetail with the emotional resonance that poetry offers?

Because I cannot offer detailed analysis here to address these questions, I will focus only on specific moments that are pertinent to our discussion of Bugis Street. Interestingly, Kaye calls his collection *Bugis Street Blues* without saying a word about Bugis Street in any of the poems included in the collection. "Bugis Street Adjacent" might have been a better title to represent his approach. The two poems that come closest geographically to Bugis Street are "Sago Street" and "Lavender Street."[5] "Sago Street" expresses the morning-after regret associated with indulging in the debauchery of the place, noting how "[w]e have all been here before" (3). "Lavender Street" turns toward the perspective of the prostitutes by somewhat humanizing their plight: "At half-past two they turn back home, / Their supple thighs are bruised and sore. / Their hungry children snatch their gains, / Expecting more" (Kaye 1955, 7). There is an observatory detachment of the sociological gaze at

---

5. In his study on prostitution in Singapore before the Second World War, James Warren offers data on the number of brothels appearing around the streets in the same vicinity: Sago Street had thirteen and Bugis Street fourteen in 1905 (Warren 2003, 45).

work here, mixed in with a vaguely sympathetic condescension. Could one account for this ambivalence in the resentment of the opening poem "The Expatriate," where the speaker points out how "In early manhood I am come, / Having no arts but a second-rate brain, / . . . to Singapura I am come, / Here in this foetid air to find / Some comfort in the salary / Commanded by a fourth-rate mind" (1)? Like Ommanney has reflected in his travel book, Kaye frames, and thus covers over, the sexual guilty pleasures that the colonial subject partakes of with a moral and institutional transcendence. But the return of the repressed haunts the collection with Bugis Street's liminality: calling the book *Bugis Street Blues* and not talking about the titular subject is to suggest the symbolic and fetishistic obsession with the street and what it signifies. Bugis Street's invisibility[6] and the fact that it still draws out a melancholic affect present both a simultaneous acknowledgment and disavowal of Bugis Street, a contradiction that permeates the colonial sexual consciousness. Ultimately, Bugis Street's overt and liminal presence in the British colonial textual archives, as exemplified by *Eastern Windows* and *Bugis Street Blues* respectively, unveils the street as a literary fabulation of colonial desire for the (sexual) conquest of and domination over the Asian Other.

Nostalgia and Queer Liberal Politics

As my search for references to Bugis Street moved to more recent online and literary texts by politically liberal white male authors, I noticed that the political motivations and framing may have

---

6. The trope of invisibility and its relation to prostitution in Singapore is not coincidental. Gerrie Lim calls his book *Invisible Trade* to discuss the presence of an elite sex trade in contemporary Singapore that is not overtly addressed in public and state discourses. See especially the chapter entitled "Boys in the Hood" for the gay aspects of this trade (Lim 2004, 105–23).

shifted, but the nostalgic obsessions with the place remain trapped in an imperial gaze. In other words, Bugis Street functions as a meme (if I may deploy new media parlance) for the Western sexual adventurism that is projected onto Asia, as both real and imaginary spaces that embody the dangers of erotic play and fantasy. I use the term "nostalgic" strategically not only to convey the fantastical glow with which Bugis Street has been imbued, a place buzzing with sexual electricity, but also in the theoretical way Rey Chow has approached the concept of nostalgia: "[I]nstead of thinking that nostalgia is a feeling triggered by an object lost in the past (a mode of thinking that remains linear and teleological in orientation), could we attempt the reverse? Perhaps nostalgia is a feeling looking for an object? If so, how does it catch its object? Could the movement of nostalgia be a loop, a throw, a network of chance, rather than a straight line?" (Chow 1998, 135). In my brief analysis of two texts involving Bugis Street—American author James Eckardt's *Singapore Girl: A True Story of Sex, Drugs and Love on the Wild Side in 1970s Bugis Street* (2006) and the semi-anonymous Bob from Australia's "The Sailor's Birthday Present" that appeared in Alex Au's blog *Yawning Bread*—I ask how Bugis Street becomes the reconstructed object of the author's nostalgic search, and how thinking along these lines helps question the ontological crisis that the nostalgic object offers white male identity.

Of the two texts, I would like to begin with the more problematic *Singapore Girl* by James Eckardt. The author's liberal background is established rather concretely in his biographical profile (in the book): as an "ex-civil rights volunteer, James Eckardt joined the Peace Corps," working in Sierra Leone and Brazil, before his "stopover in Singapore led him into the bawdy spectacle of 1970s Bugis Street—a world long vanished today." This biographical information also reaffirms his heteronormativity as "Eckardt settled in Thailand where he's lived for thirty years with his Thai wife and four children." So, *Singapore Girl* can be seen as a nostalgic attempt to capture a moment of youthful abandonment and indulgence (a time before his return to the respectability of traditional family life), when he fell in love with Milly, a transgender prostitute, to whom the book is also dedicated.

There is something to be said about the liberal chutzpah that Eckardt displays in his open-mindedness with alternative sexualities and the strong sense of security with his heterosexual manhood, permitting him to enter into the seedy world of Bugis Street and to actually fall in love with one of its transsexual occupants. Jim, as Eckardt calls himself, is streetwise enough to discern the gender performativity evident among the prostitutes he encounters:

> Parody indeed. Far more than they'd dreamed . . . [E]very whore who wiggled and gave coy inviting looks . . . each and everyone of those painted, wigged, tight-skirted whores held a secret curse tight between their legs. This was Bugis Street. (Eckardt 2006, Part 1.3)[7]

He is also astute, though brashly so, in his reading of their psychological makeup:

> So in some part of their being they could not help but hate men even as women they longed to be dominated and fucked by that very stiff uncompromising maleness they had foresworn . . . Their real interest and abiding love lay not in any man but in the woman's image that stared back at them so beautifully from their dressing table mirror. Their real eternal love was the reflected image of themselves, their consuming passion reserved only for the mirror image of illusion, makeup, costume and pose, eternal theater with actress and spectator the same person, an endless

---

7.   The kindle version of *Singapore Girl* does not display page numbers. Instead, the book has a prologue, three parts, and multiple epilogues. For citation purposes, Part 1.3 refers to Part One, Section Three.

drama on a private stage played out in the bottomless narcissistic
pools of mirror time. (Part 1.8)

But the narcissism that he sees in these prostitutes he barely sees
in himself, though some glimmer of enlightenment occasionally
breaks through. For instance, he does not view himself as a "faggot"
when he has sex with another prostitute Jackie (Part 1.8); but when
he is with Milly, he has "the sudden and perverse realization . . . that
he was fucking a boy" (Part 1.16). He seems conscientious enough to
denote his Orientalist view of Milly, who "abided in an Asian eternal
present, elemental, powerful, beyond his ken, a wonder and delight
to behold" (Part 1.12). Discursively, Milly has become Jim's own
Madame Butterfly, and he "[e]ver the man, the American, . . . was
already making plans for her" (Part 1.14), an implicit self-critique
of the cultural imperialism he is a part of. Whether fiction mirrors
reality, or reality fiction, it is deeply disturbing to hear Jim recount
the news of Milly committing suicide by jumping off one of
Singapore's HDB flats; just as Cio-Cio San kills herself when she
is abandoned by the American Lieutenant Pinkerton in Giacomo
Puccini's opera *Madama Butterfly*. It is even more troubling to hear
Jim assume responsibility for Milly's complexes by contradictorily
detaching himself from it:

> And that her true self is locked somewhere inside that mirror,
> enslaved to it, and afraid to come out, to be a real living breathing
> woman in the real world, to grapple and grow with a *real man*.
> And that Jim abetted in her narcissism, encouraged her with his
> uncritical wide-eyed adulation, his enthusiastic audience of one
> only enhanced the illusion for her. But Jim was not needed to
> maintain the illusion. The mirror was enough. (Part 2.6; emphasis
> mine)

This tone of political self-reflexivity and self-denigration is
double-edged in that, while it may be genuine, it is also protective

of the liberal, white male subject's complicity in furthering the historical dynamics of colonial cultural power that defines desire in postcolonial Asia. The sublimation of Bugis Street and Milly into the safety zone of a nostalgic past permits the narrator to luxuriate, and even repeatedly indulge, in the soft-core narrative iterations of his sexual and emotional encounters with Milly and other characters he meets in Bugis Street. One could describe the narrative structure as a continual loop that returns again and again to these eroticized moments. It is highly telling, therefore, that the overly extended text could have been revised to half its length, without losing its essential point. This indulgence is not guilt-free, of course; in fact, guilt assumes a masochistic valence as the melancholic reliving of his sexual entanglements necessitates. It comes as no surprise that the author's original intention was to write "a novel to be called *Bugis Street Blues* starring Milly and me" ("Ten Years Later"), a titular coincidence that resonates with the thematic concerns of Barrington Kaye's poetry collection. My critical intention here is not to question Eckardt's sincerity or the veracity of his memoir, or to be prudish about its overt sexuality; rather, my goal is to identify the ideological factors (of a political unconscious) that determine the narrative structuring of the book,[8] and, in turn, to understand the book's place in the larger discursive constellation defining Bugis Street.

As a productive counterpoint to Eckardt's nostalgic musings on Bugis Street, I want to offer some analytical observations on a blog essay entitled "The Sailor's Birthday Present" written by Bob from Australia and generously published by Alex Au on his blog website *Yawning Bread*. This guest essay provides a response to Au's piece "The Leech on the Trannie's Bum" regarding the matter

---

8. One could extend a similar critique to Daniel Gawthrop's *The Rice Queen Diaries: A Memoir* (Gawthrop 2005), which can be viewed as a non-Singapore, gay version of *Singapore Girl*.

of the West's obsession with Bugis Street.[9] Bob from Australia's gay perspective on Bugis Street is a refreshing one and has inclined my biases in his favor; his nostalgic memories of the place occupy a median position between Eckardt's memoir and Alex Au's critique, which I find theoretically and culturally useful.

Bob begins with an important caveat to his romanticized recollections by noting how "memory is an imperfect medium. As we age selective memory tends to overlay present insipid reality and 'the older I get the better I was' syndrome kicks in" (Bob from Australia 2002), a self-conscious reflection that parallels Eckardt's. But even when Bob tries "to keep it as factual as possible," he "can assure you that Bugis St was raunchy enough then not to need artistic license to make it sound titillating now." And titillate Bob's account does, like many of the other narratives that reference Bugis Street, though not in the same way that one has come to expect. Bob surprises his reader with a story of how he met, while spending time at Bugis Street, not a transgender Singapore prostitute, but instead a British sailor whom he describes as "a rather spunky blonde who . . . was magnificent":

> Hair the colour of ripe corn spilling out from under a cap on back of head, six foot of nordic manhood as only the Brits & Scandinavians can do it and a cheeky grin looking up at me as he sprawled at the table. I think my lifelong passion for sailors & foreskins (he had a beyooootiful one) joined an existing passion for Asia on that night and none of them have ever left me.

With the help of a resourceful taxi driver who knew the city well, the two men culminated their sexual rendezvous in the manner many pornographic narratives eventually do.

Let me enumerate the number of ways his account challenges the ideological assumptions of previous accounts and refigures

---

9. For my own take on Au's essay, see pages 2–4 of this book.

Bugis Street as a cultural space for political resistance and rethinking: (1) the racialized narrative twist disturbs the Orientalist paradigm of the straight/gay white male fetishism of the feminized Asian Other—neither am I here denying the important subjective reality and consciousness of transgender individuals (a point that I address in earnest in Chapter 3), nor am I suggesting that a white-on-white sexual connection is the only cultural political option to disentangle the complexities of interracial desire. (2) Bob retains his (sexual) desire for Asia and Asians in a way that indicates the heterogeneous forms and practices of queer sexualities, which refuse strict racial and, at times, racist typology—he facetiously inquires of Alex Au if he could be introduced to someone who might fulfill his "ideal of a red headed Asian sailor with tattoos & a foreskin." (3) He historicizes and appreciatively confronts the redrawn lines of racial and cultural power in contemporary Singapore that accounts for the confluence between racial and, now, class oppression in a transnational capitalist era. He does so by first acknowledging his (neo)colonial complicity by noting how "[w]e (whites) used to be able to patronize you but we can't do that any more which pleases me. Although I accepted it, I was always troubled that I could go places & do things in Asia purely because I was a white man even though it was your country!" Next, he couples, courageously and necessarily, this white liberal guilt with a critique of the Asian capitalist elite for taking the place of the former colonialist in exploiting a widening wealth gap in many Asian countries—"It troubles me still that the emergent middle class in Asia seems now to be in retreat and there is a return to the previous pattern where people are either obscenely wealthy or grindingly poor with not much in between. In spite of the American Imperium, I still think this century will be an Asian one and I hope you guys will make a better fist of it than did my generation." And, finally, (4) he strategically imbues Bugis Street with a nostalgic spirit of "good humour, even bonhomie," while admitting "that rosy recollection may alter reality." Therefore, Bugis Street embodies, or becomes metonymic of, human sociality and connectedness that is possible in spite of, or maybe even because of, the sexual congress that the geographical space once permitted and encouraged. This fabulation of a humanized and humane Bugis Street, one that embraces its goodness and its flaws, its possibilities and it failures, will later become central in my readings of Yonfan's cinematic turn on the subject.

Bugis Street Reconstructed

The processes of urban renewal in Singapore form a story of modernity that is marked by sharp twists and turns. The economic pragmatism that drove the major spatial and architectural redevelopment projects in the central business district and its surrounding areas soon exposed the cultural shortsightedness of its proponents. The antiseptic "cleansing" of Chinatown and Bugis Street in the 1980s, for instance, led to the loss of their cultural charm and "authenticity" that attracted tourists to them in the first place. The economic pragmatist logic, which once had argued for the destruction of the old, looped around to propound for the necessity of cultural and heritage preservation. But how does one conjure that which has somewhat organically evolved in Singapore's history without resorting to a certain degree of museumized reconstruction or Disney-style mimicry? What slippages occur in this cultural, architectural, and geographical remaking? What gets projected into its place as markers of authenticity and what, in turn, gets displaced? Because of the multiple attempts at reviving the atmosphere and spirit of Bugis Street in the past two decades, it is beyond my ability as a non-historian to examine the intricate incarnations that the revived Bugis Street has physically assumed.

Instead, for the purposes of this chapter, I turn to two televisual representations of these reconstructions to illustrate and theorize the ideological processes at work.[10]

The first instance is a seventeen-minute promotion video, *The New Attractions*, produced in 1990 by the Tourism Resource Centre for the Singapore Tourism Board, a state-run entity. This short documentary offers a survey of the various sights that tourists can expect to encounter when they visit Singapore, Bugis Street being one of those locations. The segment features a series of still photographs, while offering viewers a montage of aerial view shots of Bugis Street, as it underwent urban renewal. These aerial shots obviously deny us close-up images of the "risqué" that the narrator touts:

> Another example of vintage wine in a very new bottle is the reborn Bugis Street, carefully modeled on the original naughty but much loved Bugis Street. The new Bugis Street is still a tantalizingly risqué late-night eating spot where the intermingling of aromas, gaudy colors, and near pandemonium noise level provides the same floating sensations of its famous predecessor.[11]

This montage sequence is followed by another one of food hawker stalls displaying their wares. It is obvious that the exoticism of food—the state here cashing in on Singapore's multicultural cornucopia of gastronomic delights as the reliable stand-in for the touristic attraction to cultural difference—has strategically replaced the exoticism of the sexually risqué. But what is being displaced does inevitably return to haunt. The erotics of food that once comingled with the erotics of sexual temptations now only traces

---

10. I would like to thank the National Archives of Singapore for granting me access to copies of these two television programs.

11. *The New Attractions*, Singapore Tourism Board, U-matic (Video), Singapore, 1990.

the latter's voluptuous contours and, thereby, its absence. This tracing accentuates sexuality's disappearance and sublimation: prostitution and queer sexualities have been driven into the liminal spaces of Singapore polite society's visual periphery. The olfactory, visual, and auditory assaults that food (as sex's replacement) offers almost, but never quite match, the "same floating sensations" of sexual *jouissance*. It is almost the "same" but not quite.

State-run media in Singapore keeps following the same tack with Bugis Street, even as recently as 2004 with SPH Media Works' production of the second series of *Site and Sound with Julian Davidson*. In Episode Four, inappropriately titled "In Between a Beach and Queen," British presenter Davidson strolls with the viewers through Bugis Junction, the first air-conditioned street that was turned into a shopping mall. The narrator sets an unusual tone, for Singapore television programming that is, by acknowledging, albeit obliquely, the flawed state policies on urban renewal of the recent past. "But whereas the street plan might have been loosely maintained," he intones, "the shop-houses lining Bugis, Hylam, Malay, and Malabar Streets were not. Admittedly, what replaced them was a sincere and practical attempt to recreate the past. However, the fact is not a single brick remains of what once originally occupied this entire historical city block. It's rather a pity that just a couple of the original buildings couldn't have been incorporated into this attractive complex to provide future generations with a sense of historical continuity. But perhaps prevailing wisdom was that what went on here was best forgotten."[12] What the narrator is subtly suggesting is that this "prevailing wisdom" has decided that the geographical "censorship" of Bugis Street and its denizens will best serve future generations of Singaporeans and tourists alike. It is critical that the producers have chosen the British Julian Davidson

---

12. "In Between a Beach and Queen," *Site and Sound with Julian Davidson*, Series Two, Episode Four, SPH Media Works, DVD, Singapore, 2004.

to grant viewers a glimpse into a re-imagined past, a racialized form of nostalgic licensing to enter into this naughty world that is deemed foreign to the supposedly prim and proper Singaporean mainstream. The following dialogue between Davidson and the narrator teases viewers with a peek-a-boo effect, tantalizing them with details that they can neither confirm nor experience on their own:

Davidson: "Admittedly, the old Bugis Street may not have been everybody's cup of tea, but I personally have rather good memories of that nefarious location. It was August 1978, and the American navy was in town, the aircraft carrier USS *Enterprise* no less. You may not know this, but the American navy is actually a dry fleet, which is to say not a drop of alcohol is allowed on their ship. Well, you can imagine what happens when 630 American sailors get into town and they make a beeline for Bugis Street, or Boogie Street as they like to call it. And of course the whole world was there to meet them, every hustler, every conman, every good-time girl. And a lot of girls who, quite frankly, weren't girls at all. They just wanted to meet those thirsty American sailors. And of course awful lot of liquid refreshment went down their throats and I'm not talking orange juice. Anyway, I have to say it was probably one of the best parties I have ever been to. Like something out of a movie. And it went on all night. I'm afraid today's Bugis Street is but a pale reflection. You should have been there. Perhaps you were." . . .

Narrator: "Although Bugis Street had effectively ceased to exist, an attempt was made to preserve its spirit across the road. Shifted and sanitized, its lively and perverse charm didn't survive the transplant operation. Bugis Village is admittedly a very busy and very successful conglomeration of stores, shops, and food outlets, and undeniably a popular place to visit. But to, in any way, connect it to the Bugis Street of the past would require a quantum leap of the imagination. Right, Julian?"

Davidson: "Instead of forbidden fruit, we have forbidding fruit. Durian. And the only saucy surprises left are the sambal dishes at the food court."

Again, the cultural strategy is to contain the adult-rated Bugis Street within the nostalgic recollections of the British presenter, and to offer a PG-rated version that leaves much to the imagination. Like in *The New Attractions*, food assumes here the closest thing to erotic piquancy and intrigue that the Singapore viewer will ever get to experience of Bugis Street. This peek-a-boo effect that the program deploys only exposes the patriarchal state's distrust of and patronizing attitude toward its charge, the Singaporean viewer, whose ethical and moral "adolescence" demands state supervision. My interpretation of *Bugis Street*'s sexual visualities in Chapter 3 argues for the film's political resistance against this mode of media control.

Bugis Street Reclaimed

The archive that I have assembled so far is weighted heavily on a colonial and Western cultural imperial perspective, and understandably so, considering the timeframe that the "original" Bugis Street was organically conceived. These representations are also trapped in a historical past and, thus, can only be nostalgically memorialized or fabulated as part of specific ideological and cultural fantasies. This is and always will be the nature of Bugis Street's ontological and epistemological present and future. But one can take heart that such an understanding of Bugis Street's cultural fate need not necessarily be entirely negative or consistently problematic. My sense is that if enlightened cultural producers are willing to tap into Bugis Street's potential for the creation of politically progressive modes of multimedia semiotics and aesthetics, a fabulated Bugis Street can be reclaimed for critical resistance and intervention.

Two texts that fit this bill have emerged, rather coincidentally (or, one could argue, rather symptomatically of the era's fixations) around the same time in the mid-1990s: Yonfan's film in 1995 and Singaporean journalist/literary author Koh Buck Song's *Bugis Street: The Novel* in 1994.[13]

Two observations on the notion of historicity need to be made about *Bugis Street: The Novel* in terms of its publication format. Firstly, Koh included near the end of the book a historical section entitled "Bugis Street–A History" (Koh 1994, 157–61), indicating the historical underpinnings of his novel and, thus, the truth integrity of its contextual and historical referencing. Secondly, the novel proper, when juxtaposed against the brief history that follows, hence, presents an aestheticized critical commentary on the cold objectivity of this history, layering it with humanity in all its wonderful richness and contradictory flaws. The novel achieves this complexity by filtering Bugis Street through the multicolored lenses of individual characters involved in the central narrative drama that is unfolding. Each chapter is devoted to a specific character's perspective, which Koh rather expertly sutures together into a linear narrative that does not sacrifice the individual nuances each of the characters brings to our understanding of Bugis Street. The key protagonist Mei-li has three chapters, including the opening and closing ones. Her love interest Siong-wei has one chapter, her father Robert Ho two, her mother Mrs. Ho one, and, most significantly, Rosie (the transsexual prostitute) has an entire chapter.

---

13. A significant side note is that the novel's authorship is credited, as indicated on its main credit page, to Koh Buck Song, but "in collaboration with Tan Hwee Hua." The back page biographical profile indicates that Tan wrote the lyrics to *Bugis Street—The Musical*, a work that, to the best of my knowledge, has not been published and is, I surmise, probably the basis for this novel. *Bugis Street—The Musical*, hence, can potentially be a third text that I could have included in this chapter's final section, if it were easily and readily accessible.

While Rosie's story is critical to help further the plot of Mr. Ho's hand in her death, Koh could potentially have left it out for narrative economy. The fact that he did not is crucial in appreciating how Rosie's confessions of her desires to be a biological woman become a necessary aspect of Koh's historicized reconstruction of this social and human space that Bugis Street definitely was. The reader gets a sense of what Rosie's life was like and what drove her toward her choices, even the pains that she experienced and the courage with which she faced them: "I know I hurt Mum and Sis very much. But what can I do? I can't help it if what I want to be is not what other people want for me. After all, it's my life, not theirs . . . All of society shows no pity for people like us" (Koh 1994, 123).[14] On the one hand, if I must complain about Koh's construction of the Rosie narration, it would be the way he deployed some simplistic pop psychology about transgenderism to inhabit his character's consciousness, a method which frames Rosie according to an objectifying anthropological gaze. Also, the erasure of Rosie as transsexual subject through her death (like in Eckardt's telling of Milly's story in *Singapore Girl*) is a clichéd plot element—queer deaths being a tiresomely sad narrative trope in both literary and filmic scenarios.[15] Her death is further symbolic of the eventual

14. "People Like Us" was a queer Singaporean expression that preceded American Idol Kelly Clarkson's 2012 song of the same name. (Clarkson, of course, is riding the coattails of Lady Gaga in the latter's version of gay affirmation: "Born This Way.") "People Like Us," or PLU, is also a moniker for a gay activist group that was particularly vibrant in Singapore in the 1990s, of which Alex Au (of *Yawning Bread*) was also a part. For more information, see Lo and Huang (2003), or visit the PLU website at http://www.plu.sg/society/.

15. From a cinematic standpoint, see Vito Russo's *The Celluloid Closet* (1987) for Hollywood examples. Even in contemporary films on the subject, *Brokeback Mountain* (2005) and *A Single Man* (2009) come quickly to mind. For readings on the sad fate of queer characters in Chinese cinemas, turn to Berry (2000) and Chan (2008).

dispersal and submersion of Bugis Street's transgender prostitutes into Singapore's social margins and underground. Furthermore, the heterosexual romantic narrative of Mei-li and Siong-wei, together with the familial heteronormative melodrama between the Hos and their fraught relationship with their daughter Mei-li, occupies center stage, as many of these narratives do, thereby relegating queerness to the token status of instrumental handmaiden to populate the social backdrop of the novel's narrative setting. These are critical flaws that cannot be ignored.

On the other hand, Koh's attempt to give Rosie a voice is laudable in the way it reminds one of her humanity and the material reality of her identity struggles. (One must keep in mind that this is during the 1990s in Singapore and we queers were just happy to accept any acknowledgment of cultural political presence we could receive from the mainstream.) Writing in the early 1990s about cross-dressing and the film *Tootsie* (1982), Marjorie Garber cautions us against "readings of the film" which "erase or look through the cross-dresser, wishing instead to redistribute his/her power" (Garber 1992, 7). This advice must be taken seriously if one were to accord transgender people the respected place they deserve. Koh's inclusion of Rosie in his novel is an important first step in that direction. Yonfan's *Bugis Street* will take the next step in fleshing out the sociopolitical complexities of transgender identities and sexualities in Singapore film.

2

Bugis Street as Sexuality on Screen

Screening Sex and Prostitution: Hong Kong and Singapore

In her groundbreaking work on pornography, Linda Williams makes the tantalizing claim that the pornographic propensity of the cinematic medium is part and parcel of its very nature, what she characterizes as the "frenzy of the visible." "[T]his frenzy is neither an aberration nor an excess," she argues. The "cinematic 'implantation of perversions' in ever more visible filmic bodies and in the enhanced vision of spectators goes hand in hand with the developing pleasures of the medium" (Williams 1989, 36). Varying degrees of visual directness in the representations of sex and sexual relations populate much of cinematic histories, with heterosexual and heteronormative interactions constituting the narrative framework and foundation. Even in (relatively) conservative Chinese cultures, sex finds its way into the visual landscape of cinema in forms that some would consider surprising, if not stunning. The adage that "sex sells" is obviously true when one surveys, for instance, the vast body of mainstream and independent films from Hong Kong, Taiwan, Mainland China, and Singapore. But what is more fascinating here, though, is the manner with which sex and sexuality are situated narratively and discursively, often in an attempt to legitimize, culturally and ideologically, their presence in this "frenzy of the visible."

To illustrate this specific point, I turn, very briefly, to the depiction of prostitution in Hong Kong and Singapore cinema, so as to embed Yonfan's *Bugis Street* within the ethics of filmic representation of what many hail as the oldest profession in the world. Let me start first with a classic of Shanghai silent film, Wu Yonggang's *The Goddess* (1934), which stars the queen of Chinese melodrama Ruan Lingyu playing a long-suffering mother who prostitutes herself for her son's education and wellbeing. While one could debate the political rationale of the film, it is hard to deny the efficacy of its mother-whore typology, a common feature in melodramas featuring the fallen woman or the prostitute. While this contradictory figuration, particularly in the case of *The Goddess*, spotlights the socially oppressive and unjust systems that drive women to sell their bodies as a means of survival (Harris 2008, 134), it also generates a moralizing structure that permits the maternal to encase prostitution with an ideological justification for its cinematic presence. Ruan's character could only contemplate prostitution *because* of her maternal instincts to provide for her son. I do not want to pass judgment here on the varied reasons why one chooses to become a prostitute, or to deliberate the moral/ethical conundrums that these choices produce, as important as these debates are, especially from a feminist standpoint. Instead, I wish to spotlight the narrative structuring that this cinematic typology instantiates, as a formal strategy to mitigate the visual frenzy of sex on screen. In the case of this 1934 silent film, sex between the prostitute and her male clientele is only suggestively alluded to, of course. But, as Williams has noted about its pornographic tendencies to visualize human bodies, cinema progressively forces its way into the private realm of sexuality and is entranced by the public display of sexual solicitation that prostitution entails. The mother-whore dialectic, thus, condones the audiences' voyeuristic gaze, as sex and prostitution are safely contained for viewing within the acceptable confines of a morality tale about a mother's love and her sacrifices.

As censorship practices and viewing cultures become more relaxed about sex and sexuality on screen, prostitution also presents itself as a convenient topic of choice to locate soft-core erotic imagery. The moralizing structure identified above does not diminish or disappear, but instead intensifies as the imagery increases its sexually lurid and exploitative details. Shaw Brother's *fengyue* (風月) films offer great examples of this phenomenon. Tan See Kam describes the films of this genre as those that "depict sex and desire in explicit ways" (Tan 2013, 83) and that "were a precursor to the Category III films which mushroomed after the creation of the age-based film rating system in 1988, and are now a mainstay of Hong Kong cinema" (84). Titles with prostitution as part of its narrative include *Intimate Confessions of a Chinese Courtesan* (1972), *Kiss of Death* (1973), *The Sugar Daddies* (1973), *Sex for Sale* (1974), *Women of Desire* (1974), and *The Girlie Bar* (1976).[1] In modulating the moralistic framework that one sees in Wu Yonggang's film, *Intimate Confessions of a Chinese Courtesan* and *Kiss of Death*, for instance, present sympathetic downtrodden protagonists who are enslaved into the sex trade. They fight against their oppressors within the system in order to survive and for justice, but only to die violently in the end, as morally befitting their

---

1. The Hong Kong Film Archive's publication *The Shaw Screen* (Wong 2003) offers a complete filmography of the company's productions, including an extensive body of erotic cinema.

status as tainted and fallen women in a culturally conservative (and hypocritical) Chinese society. Yet these films are also ideologically complicit in this hypocrisy by offering plot trajectories that function as moral escape routes for their (generally heterosexual male)[2] audiences to indulge in scenes of female nudity, sexual exploits, and sexual aggression. Both films feature sexually explicit and extended sequences where the women are sexually "initiated" into their trade by a variety of lecherous men.

While most of these Shaw *fengyue* films of the 1970s focus on female prostitutes, the one exception is *Sex for Sale* where the main protagonist is a young gigolo catering to rich women. According to Tan, "[i]t is the first Hong Kong film to feature a male homosexual figure overtly, in the character of a nightclub singer who falls for the young man and, out of self-hatred, eventually commits suicide. In addition to showing the impossibility of love between men, male homosexuality itself is portrayed as a 'contagious' disease" (Tan 2013, 88–89). *Intimate Confessions of a Chinese Courtesan* is the other film that throws lesbianism into the mix.[3] Queer sexuality arrives at a tangent in these films that feature heterosexual prostitution. The first Hong Kong films that I can recall tackling queer prostitution are Yonfan's *Bugis Street* and *Bishonen*. These are landmark films precisely because of Yonfan's daring in situating queer sexuality at the center of their narratives.[4] By so

---

2. The notion of the cinematic gaze is a complex one, which includes queer possibilities, even for these *fengyue* films. Spatial constrains do not permit me to develop this analytical thread here. I address the intricacies of the sexual gaze, in the case of *Bugis Street*, in Chapter 3.

3. See Tan's essay (Tan 2013) for a close analysis of this film and its remake entitled *Lust for Love of a Chinese Courtesan* (1984), both directed by Chor Yuen.

4. This is not to suggest that the director was not plagued by anxieties in tackling such taboo subjects, especially in the 1990s. After Daniel Wu had been warned (by others) about the risks of appearing in *Bishonen*, Yonfan asked

applauding these films, it would be disingenuous of me to deny the exploitative inflections that the scenes of male nudity and queer sex can embody—elements that help the films move easily through the transnational circuits of independent cinema and foreign art films. But, at the same time, it is the very uncompromising and unapologetic display of queer sex, and even queer prostitution, that elevates Yonfan's films above the majority of the *fengyue* genre of the 1970s and the Category III erotica of the 1980s and 1990s. As I argue in Chapter 3, *Bugis Street* may be playful in its campy depiction of transgender prostitutes, but it does not turn a blind eye to the horrors and tribulations that these women suffer. Yet, it disavows a moralistic framework to judge these sex workers as an ideological cover for audiences to relish the visualities of queer sex.

To round up this section, it is necessary to mention the slim body of work in Singapore cinema that includes prostitution in a significant fashion. Considering the tight censorship laws on the depiction of sex and sexuality in the country, the *fengyue* films from Hong Kong either did not make it or did not make it intact (without cuts) to Singapore. Shaw Brothers, therefore, had to calibrate its own self-censorship practices to accommodate its Singapore market. As Stephanie Chung Po-yin points out, Shaw produced "different versions of a film for different markets with varying degrees of censorship: three versions were made, the 'hottest' for the US, Europe and Japan, the 'mildest' for Singapore and Malaysia, and the 'moderate' for Hong Kong" (Chung 2003, 9). The implementation of a ratings system since July 1, 1991 allowed

---

him, "Do you regret doing this film?" To which Wu replied, "Director, if you are not afraid, why should I regret doing it?" (Yonfan 2012, 195). When they started to shoot the bath scene, Yonfan noted how he "felt embarrassed" to see Daniel Wu and Terence Yin in the bath together, despite the actors' professionalism (196). Also, in reflecting upon the main actors' open-mindedness during the shoot, Yonfan acknowledges that some people would consider the film "immoral" (197).

films with sex and violence to be screened in Singapore theaters under a restricted (R) category. But the censors had to moderate the system later by turning the R to a more conservative R(A)— "A" for "artistic"—rating because "feedback from a large majority of Singaporeans indicated they were against the screening of exploitative R-rated movies because of the perceived detrimental effect they had on the youth of Singapore" (Thulaja 2010). Hence, many of us can only now recall the brief months between July and September 1991 as an extremely short hiatus of relative cinematic freedom, since much of the Category III erotica from Hong Kong did not make it through the censor's net after September 15. The R(A) rating permitted some films to be screened in theaters within the city center, while "films being screened at . . . neighbourhood cinemas had only the 'G' or General category or the 'PG' or Parental Guidance category, to maintain a more conservative ambience in these estates where most Singaporeans live and bring up their children" (Thulaja 2010). Intriguingly, this censorship policy relies on a questionable conceptual divide between the city and the neighborhood heartland. Alfian Bin Sa'at correctly deconstructs this geographical binarism as a cultural and ideological strategy. He aligns the heartland with the notion of a "hinterland" as "the idea of a countryside that acts as a repository of certain conservative cultural and moral values, in contradistinction to the chaotic liberal relativism of the city" (Sa'at 2012, 37). The ratings system apparently is meant to shield and to protect the Singapore heartland from the supposed moral corruption of sexually explicit and ultraviolent filmic imagery. This arbitrary geographical cordon sanitaire assumes that the more cosmopolitan and educated set occupying the urban center, including Westerners working and living in Singapore, are culturally more mature in handling R(A)-rated cinematic material, vis-à-vis the local hoi polloi, whose imagined Asian conservatism and cultural political underdevelopment demand the state's parental guidance and protection.

My short detour into the politics of film censorship in 1990s Singapore is meant to highlight its impact on production in the beginnings of Singapore's film revival. Throughout much of Singapore's film production history in the 1960s to the 1990s, both local and foreign filmmakers saw the censorship hurdles as both obstacles to overcome, as well as boundaries to challenge. As a result, prostitution was a tantalizing topic to take on, with Bugis Street often assuming the notorious locale de jour.

According to Ben Slater, "[o]ne of the first films to feature the street was Guy Green's *Pretty Polly*," based on Noel Coward's short story (Slater 2014, 48). The narrative is basically a coming-of-age story (not unlike the character Lian's in *Bugis Street*) of the British girl Polly, who arrives in Singapore to experience her sexual awakening.[5] "On her final night in Singapore, Amaz [one of the main protagonists] brings her to Bugis Street, describing it as 'an evil place.' As they arrive, documentary-style shots capture the bustle of the street and its glamorous, transgender denizens" (Slater 2014, 48). Following this obscure British film is another adaptation, this time of Paul Theroux's novel: *Saint Jack* (1979), an American production directed by Peter Bogdanovich. It tells the story of the ambitions of Jack Flower and his desires to run a brothel in Singapore (Uhde and Uhde 2010, 53). Roy Tan identifies in the film "a scene of a dazzling transwoman named Bridgit Ang, playing herself, in a platinum blonde Afro chatting up a table of Western expatriates at Bugis Street" (Tan, "Bugis Street: Transgender Aspects"). The film ran into difficulties with Singapore's censorship board in 1980, receiving a ban "for 'misrepresenting' the city" (Uhde and Uhde 2010, 53). What is fascinating about this film from a queer perspective is that it also features a subplot where a visiting United States senator steps out onto Orchard Road and picks up a

---

5. See Ben Slater's blog post for a detailed analysis of this aspect of the film (Slater 2013).

gay male prostitute for sex. This is also one of those rare moments of gay sexuality in Singapore finding its way onto the big screen, in a Hollywood film no less.[6]

Part of this string of foreign cinematic "obsessions" with Bugis Street is also Yonfan's film. *Bugis Street* was among the first entries in Singapore's contemporary cinematic revival. Coincidentally, the then up-and-coming independent director Eric Khoo also released his first feature *Mee Pok Man* (1996) during the same period as *Bugis Street*, with both films taking on the subject of prostitution. *Mee Pok Man* chronicles the macabre story of a noodle-soup hawker who falls in love with a female prostitute. After she was seriously injured in an accident, he brings her to his apartment in an attempt to nurse her back to health. Unfortunately, she dies when he is having sex with her. The conjoining of prostitution and necrophilia in Khoo's film demonstrates Jan Uhde and Yvonne Ng Uhde's point that this revival of Singapore film productions focused on the "theme of 'otherness,' which has become one of the characteristics of Singapore independent cinema" (Uhde and Uhde 2010, 74). *Bugis Street* and *Mee Pok Man*, hence, blazed the trail for later films to take on the subject in various iterations. The taxi driver protagonist in the film *Perth* (2004) develops a relationship with a prostitute. *Pleasure Factory* (2007) depicts two young army guys who visit prostitutes as part of a sexual initiation process into heterosexual manhood. This film by Ekachai Uekrongtham also has strong gay inflections, aspects of which I have addressed in an earlier essay (Chan 2012, 168). The question of gay sexuality also appears in Loo Zihan's short film *Untitled* (2005), depicting the emotional travails of a young man who prostitutes himself.

---

6. I offer an analysis of this sequence elsewhere (Chan 2012, 166–67).

Theorizing Queerness

Moving from prostitution to queer sexuality on screen, I find it necessary, as a matter of academic accuracy, to devote some discursive space to my use of "queer" in this book. The term "queer" is a theoretically fraught one that carries with it cultural baggage, especially for those of us who work in Asian cultural and cinema studies. The central reason is that queerness, for more than three decades now, has been closely associated with queer theory and LGBT activism in the West. Asian scholars, critics, and activists balk at the notion that a queer sexual or gendered identity, as conceived of in Euro-American circles, has been politically celebrated as a universal form and, consequently, imposed on a range of non-heteronormative practices and cultures in non-Western countries. The common response to this essentialist discourse is to counter it with a more virulent cultural nationalist one that fights a form of essentialism with another kind: rejecting, tout court, all "Western" identity and political labels while accentuating cultural specificity and difference, vis-à-vis what is considered the West. An example of a much more nuanced approach (but no less problematic one) is Chou Wah-shan's argument that while "queer" is useful, the Chinese term *tongzhi* (同志) is better nomenclature to describe those who engage in same-sex relations and practices in Chinese cultures and communities. The term *tongzhi*, translated as "comrade," "[a]fter 1949 . . . became a friendly and politically correct term by which to address everyone in China, as it refers to the most sacred ideal of a classless society where sisters and brothers share a selfless vision of fighting for the socialist collective interest" (Chou 2000, 1–2). After it "was appropriated by a Hong Kong gay activist in 1989 for the first Lesbian and Gay Film Festival in Hong Kong," the term gained popular currency and usage (2). But Chou's definition of the term sounds suspiciously like the term "queer" with the qualifying exception that "*tongzhi* harmonizes social relationships . . . [It] subverts the mainstream culture by queering and destabilizing rather than antagonizing and essentializing the supposedly straight world" (3–4). This argument relies on the binary premise that Chinese people inherently privilege the social over the individual, and that they prefer harmony to antagonism. *Tongzhi*, therefore, eschews the "confrontation" characterizing queer activism in the West. The examples that Chou provides include "Kiss In, AIDS protests, or the 'outrageous' drag queen in the parade that are reported and distorted in the media" (5). I understand, appreciate, and accept the impetus for Chou's prescription of *tongzhi* as a better alternative,[7] but the essentialist assumptions about Chinese culture and Chineseness are particularly difficult for me, especially in terms of how one reads a transnational Hong Kong–Singapore film like *Bugis Street*. Can *tongzhi* be a better term to describe the transgender identities and sexual practices, as they playfully intersect, in a politically transgressive fashion, the multilingual and multicultural milieu of Chinese-dominated Singapore, as it is depicted in the film? Are the many "outrageous" drag queen characters that parade around in *Bugis Street* any less Chinese or Asian because of their confrontational posturing?

In approaching *Bugis Street* as transnational *queer* cinema, I do so with these theoretical tensions in mind. Firstly, I deploy "queer" as "Western" queer theory suggests because the term connotes a sexual openness, fluidity, multiplicity, and heterogeneity that the more specific terms of "gay," "lesbian," "transgender," and "bisexual," for example, do not sufficiently offer on their own. Also, as Helen Hok-Sze Leung notes in her book on queer Hong Kong cinematic and popular culture, "'queer' provides . . . [her] with an

---

7. Because of the need for a reductive description here, I am unable to fore-ground the complexity of Chou's research and theorization. His scholarship on queer sexualities in Chinese societies is ultimately significant historical work.

analytical framework to look for what denaturalizes, disrupts, or resignifies the relation conventionally drawn between gendered embodiments, erotic desire, and sexual identities" (Leung 2008, 2). Yet, I acknowledge and distance myself from the universalizing tendencies of this theoretical concept by locating my analysis and readings of *Bugis Street* within the historical and cultural specificities of postcolonial Singapore as much as possible. In any case, "queer" has progressively become a popular term in Singapore in the way that *tongzhi* has in Hong Kong and Taiwan.[8] "The influence of Western ideas and cultures on these new imaginings of Asian homoeroticism is complex," Peter A. Jackson points out. "Western gay/lesbian styles and terminology have often been appropriated as strategies to resist local heteronormative strictures and carve out new local spaces. However, these appropriations have not reflected a wholesale recreation of Western sexual cultures in Asian contexts, but instead suggest a selective and strategic use of foreign forms to create new ways of being Asian *and* homosexual" (Jackson 2001, 6). It is, therefore, ludicrous to reject a term or a concept *solely* because it originated from the West.

Secondly, considering the subject matter of *Bugis Street*, I use "queer" in tandem with "transgender" in acknowledgment of their theoretical, epistemological, experiential, and institutional distinctions, overlaps, intersections, and conflicts. As Susan Stryker correctly pronounces in her introduction to *The Transgender Studies Reader*, "[t]he emergence of transgender studies has closely paralleled the rise of queer studies, with which it has enjoyed a close and sometimes vexed relationship" (2006, 7). As part of its historical and political emergence, "transgender" has become "a 'pangender'

---

8. As Lynette J. Chua observes, "[t]he use of the term *queer* to describe or name gay activist organizations appeared more frequently after 2005. Founders of these organizations believe that *queer* has less baggage in Singapore compared with the United States and therefore see an opportunity to claim (or reclaim) the term positively for the movement" (Chua 2014, 193).

umbrella term for an imagined community encompassing transsexuals, drag queens, butches, hermaphrodites, cross-dressers, masculine women, effeminate men, sissies, tomboys, and anybody else willing to be interpolated by the term" (4). As a result, "[q]ueer studies, though putatively antiheteronormative, sometimes fails to acknowledge that same-sex object choice is not the only way to differ from heterosexist cultural norms, that transgender phenomena can also be antiheteronormative" (7). Hence, while my broader deployment of "queer" as a generalized and encompassing term draws upon the political energies of the queer-transgender relationship and alliance, my usage of "transgender" accentuates the specificities of transgender embodiment, identification, and desire. Most significantly, my analysis of *Bugis Street* as queer cinema seeks not only to be emphatically inclusive and celebratory of transgenderism in its hermeneutics, but also to mobilize, more expansively, queer readings that interact with and go beyond the transgender framework.

Thirdly, the global mobility and currency of the term "queer," while problematic, has a specific purchase in the capitalist circuits of transnational cinemas. Song Hwee Lim describes *Bugis Street, Bishonen,* and *Peony Pavilion* as a queer "trilogy [that] deals . . . with transgenderism . . . , homosexuality . . . , and lesbianism" respectively (Lim 2006, 39). Lim's singular reference to Yonfan's trilogy in his groundbreaking book *Celluloid Comrades* is significant in that he embeds Yonfan's work within the context of the rise of gay male representations in Chinese cinemas, together with films like Chen Kaige's *Farewell My Concubine* (1993), Ang Lee's *The Wedding Banquet* (1993), Wong Kar-wai's *Happy Together* (1997), and Stanley Kwan's *Lan Yu* (2001). One needs to keep in mind that the emergence of a "New Queer Cinema" in the US independent film scene could arguably have generated an appetite for queer representation, as part of an emerging, fashionable global cinematic aesthetic within international film festival cultures. It is no coincidence that both *Farewell My Concubine* and *The Wedding Banquet* were nominated in the Best Foreign Language Film category in the 1994 Academy Awards. This intersection of "artistic" cinema and queerness, together with queer cinemas' global critical and, to a certain extent, commercial success, energized a transnational, queer filmic wave in Chinese cinemas. Yonfan's trilogy rode that wave in the mid-1990s to the early 2000s. My use of "queer" to mark the place that *Bugis Street* occupies in this transnational phenomenon is to complicate queer sexuality's politically progressive potential with its complicity in global capitalist transactions.

And, finally, and most importantly, my use of "queer" in this book is political in its strategy. In negotiating the concept of a queer Chinese cinema, Song Hwee Lim warns us against "the assumption that the category of queer is necessarily more progressive . . . Rather, the term 'queer,' not unlike the terms 'homosexuality' and 'Chineseness,' can equally be mobilized in essentialized ways to exclude and stigmatize those whom it otherwise claims to embrace and celebrate" (Lim 2006, 184). Lim's plea is basically for one not to be theoretically sloppy and lazy in the usage of the term, but to be conscientious and self-reflective in the manner with which the term is mobilized for specific political reasons. While I am painfully cognizant of the prescriptive dangers of a category like "transnational queer cinema," I accept the risks because of the strategic potential that such a mode of reading offers in this book. My analysis in Chapters 3 and 4 mobilizes the potential of viewing *Bugis Street* as a queer cultural text that intervenes and engages, transnationally I might add, the politics of queer sexuality and gender in Singapore.

Screening Transgender

The perception of Chinese cultural conservatism has defined the way queer sexual and gendered imagery on cinematic screens is constructed, censored, and circulated in Hong Kong and Singapore. Of course, the colonial and postcolonial histories of these two countries have also played a crucial role in shaping social attitudes toward non-heteronormative sexualities and genders, which in turn color the way cinemas thematize them, if at all. Because both Hong Kong and Singapore were once under British colonial rule, the criminalization of homosexuality constitutes an unfortunate chapter in their histories. The criminalization of sodomy and male homosexual practices went into effect through the English Offenses Against Persons Act of 1861, which the colonial government applied to the Hong Kong territories in 1865 (Chou 2000, 61). Residing in Sections 49 and 51 of the Chapter "Abominable Offense" within the Offense Against Persons Ordinance of 1901 are the horrifically harsh laws in question—Section 49 states that "[a]ny person who is convicted of the abominable crime of buggery, committed with mankind or with any animal, shall be guilty of a felony, and shall be liable to imprisonment for life"; while Section 51 goes even further by establishing how "[a]ny male person who, in public or private, commits or is party to the commission of, or procures or attempts to procure the commission by any male person of any act of gross indecency with another male person shall be guilty of a misdemeanor [*sic*] triable summarily and shall be liable to imprisonment for 2 years" (quoted in Chou 2000, 61–62). Though decriminalization finally occurred in Britain in 1967, the same did not result in its Hong Kong colony until much later in 1991 (Chou 2000, 75–78).[9] Similar laws can still be found in Singapore, despite the nation

9. See Chou Wah-shan's detailed accounting of this road to decriminalization, especially the impact that the MacLennan case and the 1997 British handover of Hong Kong had on the laws (Chou 2000, 66–78).

gaining its independence from British colonial rule in 1965. Also inherited from the colonial British legal system, Singapore law has retained the criminalization of sodomy under Section 377A of the Penal Code, in spite of recent mobilizations of grassroots political activism against its basic infringement of human rights. Section 377A basically states that "[a]ny male person who in public or private commits or abets the commission of, or procures or attempts to procure the commission of any male person of any act of gross indecency with another male person shall be punished with imprisonment for a term which may extend to two years" (quoted in Ng 2003, 18).[10] This law and the propagation of homophobic and transphobic discourses in Singapore not only function as the backdrop for queer cinema, but they also constitute a conservative bulwark of bigoted thinking against which *Bugis Street* and other queer films in varying degrees confront and struggle.

The histories of lesbian and gay representations and themes in Chinese films within Hong Kong and Singapore (and even in Taiwan, Mainland China, and the Chinese diaspora, particularly as they intersect and influence work in Hong Kong and Singapore) are impractical to replay here within the confines of this chapter.[11] Instead, I have chosen to map thematically and selectively the terrain of transgender depictions in Hong Kong and Singapore cinemas, so as to set up the contexts for my readings of *Bugis Street* in Chapters 3 and 4.

---

10. The complex impact and effect that this law has had on queer cultures are clearly beyond the scope of this book. I can only suggest to the reader Audrey Yue and Jun Zubillaga-Pow's edited collection of essays *Queer Singapore* for further illumination (Yue and Zubillaga-Pow 2012). For the legal aspects of the issue, see particularly Michael Hor's chapter.

11. Readers should turn to the work of Chris Berry (2000; 2001), Helen Hok-Sze Leung (2008; 2010), Song Hwee Lim (2006), and Fran Martin (2003b; 2010), for instance. For a brief study of queer Singapore cinema, see my essay (Chan 2012).

The representational convention of gender transgression in cinema usually assumes the form of the "comedic" figure of the "sissy" as the convenient shorthand for gay men. In his examination of Hollywood's exploitation of the effeminate male on screen, Vito Russo posits that "the creation of the sissy [was] inevitable" to shore up the hetero-masculinity of the "real man." But the result of which is that "the danger of gayness . . . lurked always in the background" (Russo 1987, 6). The humor that this character typology supposedly promises has filmmakers repeatedly returning to it for tacky and offensive comic relief, a method that Hong Kong[12] and Singapore directors are also guilty of. Another subspecies of this figuration is the male-to-female cross-dresser, a popular version being the one where a male character, accidentally or unintentionally, is forced to adopt female dress to get out of a sticky situation. These kinds of plot scenarios are only interesting to the extent that they spectacularly display, in cinematic form, the homophobia and the transphobia that have permeated public and cultural consciousness.

In the context of traditional Chinese culture, cross-dressing affords an additional valence that lifts the gendered practice out of the realm of humorous entertainment. Chinese operatic conventions on film have permitted and even celebrated both female-to-male and male-to-female cross-dressing. The *Huangmei* opera film (黃梅調), for instance, is a genre that has played with complex gender crossings and identifications. A beautiful example is the Shaw production *The Love Eterne* (1963) featuring the classic story of Liang Shanbo and Zhu Yingtai. The actress Ivy Ling Po assumed the role of the male scholar Liang Shanbo, while Betty Loh Ti played his lover. To complicate matters further on a diegetic level, Zhu also cross-dresses as another male scholar within the narrative. Tan See Kam and Annette Aw theorize "that viewers at

---

12. For a list of Hong Kong films in the 1990s that configure "sissies" as stand-ins for gay men, see Kong (2005, 66).

the time accepted cross-sex acting in films" to the point where male audiences "perceived Ling as a woman while women perceived her as a man after watching her performance as Liang Shanbo" (Tan and Aw 2008, 161). The transgender potential of opera on film has probably inspired Yonfan to insert sonic sequences of the *Kunqu* (崑曲) opera *Peony Pavilion* into his film of the same name, to allow the masculine character Lan (Joey Wang) to express her love for Jade (Rie Miyazawa). Boys and men playing female roles in Chinese opera also provided the premise for Chen Kaige's *Farewell My Concubine*, which helped generate a global interest in queer sexualities in Chinese cinema during the early 1990s, hence paving the way for a film like *Bugis Street*.

The period from the late 1980s to the mid-1990s saw the proliferation of transgender characters in *wuxia pian* (武俠片, martial arts films) and, what Stephen Teo has described as, *wuxia shenguai* films (武俠神怪, the hybrid martial art–supernatural films) (Teo 2009, 27).[13] The key figure responsible for this trend is director/producer Tsui Hark. Directing films such as *Peking Opera Blues* (1986) and *The Lovers* (1994) and taking on producer duties in his collaborations with director Ching Siu-Tung in *A Chinese Ghost Story* (1987), *Swordsman II* (1992), and *Swordsman III: The East Is Red* (1993), Tsui Hark developed a checkered reputation for thrusting cross-dressing and cross-gender transmogrification into the Hong Kong cinematic spotlight. Featuring the director's work in his documentary *Yang ± Yin: Gender in Chinese Cinema* (1998), Stanley Kwan enacts a standard critique of this series of transgender characters and imagery: "Tsui often starts from questions of gender and sexuality. But his endings always reaffirm heterosexual orthodoxy. The subversion is defused. Since his endings are always

---

13. Kong offers an excellent discussion of the different modes and dynamics of cross-dressing in Hong Kong cinema, especially films from the 1980s and 1990s, including and beyond the martial arts genre (2005, 68–71).

so resolutely heterosexual, I wondered why Tsui is so drawn to confusions of sex and gender in the first place?" When interviewed by Kwan, Tsui explains:

> *Swordsman II* is about a transsexual. But if you ask about gender confusions in general, I don't know, maybe it's to do with what we went through in the 60s. There were so many movements. Gay rights, women's lib, Black civil rights. Everyone was fighting for their own corner and their own rights. Some gay films are touching not because they're gay, but because of their humanity. Everyone has the right to be whatever they [*sic*] want.

Hence, even if the imagery is questionable, if not objectionable, what Tsui Hark has done is to bring transgender bodies into filmic visibility. Of course, some of the imagery can be outright disturbing, such as the monstrous villain in *A Chinese Ghost Story* called Madam. "While the script does not include any mention of Madam's gender history," Helen Hok-Sze Leung observes, "the casting of male actor Lau Siu-ming in the role uses the audience's nondiegetic recognition of a male body to suggest a discrepancy between male body and feminine presentation." This "titillating sight of her gender ambiguity [functions] as a physical manifestation of . . . her monstrosity" (Leung 2012, 188), just as her giant phallic tongue penetrates and consumes her male victims while they are in the throes of heterosexual passion. The transgendered being is thus embodied as otherworldly and nonhuman.

But, in a different critical turn, Leung productively reclaims Tsui Hark's work in a counterintuitive analysis of Brigitte Lin's appearances as the gender-bending *Dongfang Bubai* (東方不敗) in *Swordsman II* and *Swordsman III: The East Is Red*, by reading the films against the grain of Jin Yong's novel (upon which the films are based). "Conceived as a symbol of masculinity under threat by a transphobic imagination during the 1960s, Dongfang Bubai is emerging in the new millennium as a transsexual icon," Leung writes (2008, 73).[14] As this transsexual icon, Brigitte Lin exudes an androgynous beauty that has clearly transfixed many a director. Wong Kar-wai cast Lin in the brother-sister roles of Murong Yin (慕容嫣)/ Murong Yang (慕容燕) in *Ashes of Time* (1994). Yonfan himself expressed deep admiration for the star by describing her as "this dominating beauty [who] looks like she can exercise magical powers" (Yonfan 2012, 156). He even convinced her to lend her voice as narrator in both *Bishonen* and *Peony Pavilion*, which, according to Tony Williams, "intuitively represents Lin's now established gender-blurring star persona . . . [and] significantly associates her with feminist definitions concerning the role of the off-screen voice" (2010, 148). The iconicity of Lin's star persona as embodied in these roles elevates her as a queer diva, like a divine being, larger than life, with a luminescent *trans*cendence, beyond gender fixity. She is in the same league as the queer-identified, classic Hollywood female icons like Marlene Dietrich, Bette Davis, Barbara Stanwyck, Greta Garbo, Gloria Swanson, and Joan Crawford. The camp aesthetic of this diva iconicity Yonfan adopts for transgender characters like Lola and Drago in *Bugis Street*.

Despite the fact that *Bugis Street* is a lesser-known title of Hong Kong cinema, it is a significant film at that time because it allowed transgender prostitution to, unflinchingly, take center stage in filmic narrative. One can make a similar claim for the film in terms of its place within the Singapore canon. As in Hong Kong, transgender individuals in Singapore inhabit the margins of society and on screen. Effeminate men, male transvestites, and male-to-female transsexuals have been derogatorily referred to as *ah gua*, a colloquial Singapore term that has yet been reclaimed in an empowering fashion by the transgender community the way

---

14. For a closer analysis of these films that emphasize transgender subjectivity and embodiment, see Leung (2005).

"queer" has been in the West. Another negative descriptive label is *renyao* (人妖), which in Mandarin denotes and connotes a nonhuman abjection—with *ren* meaning human, and *yao* referring to nonhuman entities, as in *yaojing* (妖精, monstrous supernatural beings). The linguistic inhabitation of this abject space between human and nonhuman parallels the manner with which many transgender subjects occupy the margins or the interstitial spaces of mainstream Singapore society. It also legitimizes, in the transphobic perspective, the inhumane treatment that transgender subjects frequently suffer. Despite its outsized notoriety and its objectification as touristic spectacle, the historical Bugis Street was one such marginal space. Interestingly, Yonfan's original Chinese title for *Bugis Street* was "三畫二郎情" (Yonfan 2012, 146), which can be roughly translated as "Three Pictures and an Affair between Two Men." While Yonfan used the original title in the Singapore release, it was changed to 妖街皇后 for Hong Kong distribution. The revised title's literal translation is "Queen of *Yao* Street," with *yao* referring to *renyao*. This Chinese title echoes another Hong Kong film about prostitution, *Queen of Temple Street* (廟街皇后) (1990), starring Sylvia Chang,[15] which could explain Yonfan's choice of the current title. But the deployment of *yao* with its derogatory valence is still a baffling and troubling one, considering Yonfan's liberal attitude toward queer sexualities and genders. In the 2015 installment of his memoir, the director acknowledges this contradictory point when he describes how the Singapore media's obsessive and repeated use of the term *renyao* in relation to the film provoked transgender viewers to ask the production company to deal with this issue. Their appeal to the humanity of transgender people pivots on the word *ren*, hence distancing themselves from the derogatory word *yao* (Yonfan 2015, 21). It is, therefore, to

---

15. I would like to thank the anonymous reviewer of my manuscript for pointing out this allusion.

Yonfan's credit that he has restored the original Chinese title in the remastered version *Bugis Street Redux*, which was featured at the 62nd Berlin International Film Festival in 2012.[16]

The ironic disjuncture between the political spectacle of drag and the state's belief (in collusion with society's transphobia) in constraining and confining this performativity and its presence has resulted in the production of containment fields within the popular cultural realm. Kumar, one of Singapore's best-known drag performers, did not cross-dress on television shows, but only performed in drag within the (quasi-)safe confines of his cabaret venue Boom Boom Room.[17] The cabaret bar scene is, hence, seen as a more restricted venue where only a very limited number of the viewing public can access such subversive gender-bending playfulness. The theater art scene has also an equivalent cordoning effect. Ivan Heng's cross-dressed version of Stella Kon's *Emily of Emerald Hill* could only reach a select group of theater aficionados and enthusiasts, with the prohibitive theater ticket prices ruling out a broad swath of mainstream audiences (Chan 2004, 32). If cross-dressing were ever to appear on television or mainstream cinema, it would be sanitized and sexually neutralized, like in actor/director Jack Neo's early work as the lovable grandmother character Liang Po Po. The initial incarnation of this character started out as a humorous character skit in 1990s television.[18] Her popularity grew

16. Email correspondence with director Yonfan, March 18, 2015.

17. Watch a documentary produced by Vasantham Central channel called "Kumar: Truth or Dare" (2006). The program is now available in three parts on YouTube at https://www.youtube.com/watch?v=iye-AtvxiIg, accessed January 30, 2015.

18. Kenneth Paul Tan identifies the local television variety show featuring Liang Po Po to be *Comedy Night* (2008, 159). Though his analysis of Jack Neo's career mostly highlights the Chinese cultural ideological bent of the director's films, Tan isolates a transgender and queer moment in Neo's first film *Money No Enough* (1998) where "effeminacy and homosexuality are . . . portrayed

to the extent that she was given her own feature film entitled *Liang Po Po: The Movie* (1999). As innocuous and family-friendly as this figure may seem, Neo's character is an ageist and sexist depiction of geriatric, female bumbling. Neo's heterosexual masculinity is never in question, as the humorous feminized skin of Liang Po Po could not quite fully contain Neo's awkward masculine edges. One may compare his performance to Jack Lemmon in *Some Like It Hot* (1959), Dustin Hoffman in *Tootsie* (1982), and Robin Williams in *Mrs. Doubtfire* (1993), but without the commanding acting finesse of these Hollywood legends. It is in this context of cultural and institutional censorship and confinement that one finds Yonfan's *Bugis Street* subversive and challenging. Because of the film's subject matter and its brazen sexual imagery, the Board of Film Censors gave *Bugis Street* an R(A) rating at the time of its premiere, hence basically limiting its geographical scope of theatrical screenings to the city center and denying it later VCD and DVD release to the general public. Hence, local audiences' access to queer Singapore films is often dependent on illegal pirated copies or through Internet sales—*Bugis Street* is currently available through Yonfan's personal website.[19] The film, therefore, exemplifies a cultural political trend in an alternate cinematic history, which I have theorized as an "impossible presence" (Chan 2012). My deployment of this trope is to pinpoint the liminal materiality of queer Singapore cinema's illusive presence on local theater screens and Singapore audiences' difficult, if not impossible, access to commercial copies of these works within the context of the state's

---

. . . as both cultural threats and objects of ridicule" in their alignment with Westernization, hence allowing the film to imply "that Westernized Chinese men should be feared and ridiculed as degenerate: a corruption of original and authentic Chinese identity and values" (2008, 155). Jeremiah Adolpher Lee, the character who is the object of this ridicule and who appears in a dream segment in drag, is coincidentally played by Ernest Seah, *Bugis Street*'s Lola.

19. See Introduction, footnote 9.

strict film censorship laws. *Bugis Street* must be credited for blazing a trail for queer and transgender subjectivities to find their representational counterparts on Singapore screens, as we now see in works like Glen Goei's *Forever Fever* (1998)—which has a transsexual subplot—Lim May Ling's documentary *Women Who Love Women* (2006), and Kan Lume and Loo Zihan's *Solos* (2007), Singapore's first gay feature film.

3

Bugis Street as Transnational Queer Cinema

Introduction: Queer Existential Crisis

Yonfan's film *Bugis Street* begins with a textual epigraph from Shakespeare's *Hamlet*: "To be or not to be, that is the question." The citation of this classic (and probably most quoted) opening line from Hamlet's famous soliloquy is a standard, if not clichéd, signaling of existential crisis. The situational gravitas of ontological consideration—as a suicidal Hamlet debates if it is "nobler in the mind to suffer / The slings and arrows of outrageous fortune, / Or to take arms against a sea of troubles, / And by opposing end them? To die . . ." (Act 3, Scene 1)[1]—appears, at first glance, to be an incongruent way to open a playful, campy,[2] and melodramatic film about transgender prostitutes in Singapore. One mode of

---

1. I am citing from the following online version of Shakespeare's play: http://shakespeare.mit.edu/hamlet/full.html.

2. Jason Ho Ka-Hang dissects the camp aesthetics of Yonfan's cinema, particularly *Color Blossoms* and *Bishonen* (2012, 291–98).

reading this odd pairing is to see how the epigraph foregrounds the serious question of queer existence in Singapore, as the political and philosophical backdrop of the film. Lesbian, gay, bisexual, and transgender communities and activists have suffered and continue to suffer a threat to their public visibility at the hands of homophobic social and cultural forces, and of an antiquated anti-sodomy law.[3] The disappearance of the historical Bugis Street has become the signifying trope for the closeting of queer lives and the presence of liminal spaces for queer communities. Therefore, the concept of visibility plays a crucial role in the political narration of queer existence in Singapore, as it has for queer activism in many nations in the West. At the beginning of his important essay "Tiptoe Out of the Closet: The Before and After of the Increasingly Visible Gay Community in Singapore," Russell Heng reconstructs Bugis Street as one of two proto-queer sites of Singapore's "gay scene"—the other being gay bars around Orchard Road in the 1970s—which offer only a limited "lifestyle" alternative in terms of sexual identity (Heng 2001, 83). Heng's incorporation of Bugis Street into his historical narrative functions as a necessary rhetorical pivot for him to argue for increasing the visibility of queer activism and communities as the political path forward.[4]

---

3. See Chapter 2 for my brief discussion of Section 377A of Singapore's Penal Code.

4. Heng complicates the Singapore situation by arguing thus: "the gay struggle in most western societies took place within well established [*sic*] liberal democratic polities where there was a strong tradition and acceptance of political activism . . . In Singapore, which basically is still an authoritarian country, these liberties cannot be taken for granted. Top down institutional intolerance for dissent, or its lack of, is only half the problem. The other half is the lack of a constituency, with possibly a majority of gay people still being uncomfortable about a more assertive form of gay activism" (Heng 2001, 95–96). In recent years, Singapore's queer consciousness is on the threshold of a radical shift for a new generation brought up on new media technologies. The Pink Dot movement is an excellent example of this rejuvenated

Another hermeneutical turn on the intersectional focus of queer existence and political visibility that I can offer is for one to read Yonfan's delightfully excessive film as brushing up, in its comedic capacity, against its own philosophically weighty epigraph, in embrace of this point of contradiction as a mode of cinematic intervention and disidentification. In disidentification I am thinking specifically of José Esteban Muñoz's theoretical formulation:

> Disidentification is meant to be descriptive of the survival strategies the minority subject practices in order to negotiate a phobic majoritarian public sphere that continuously elides or punishes the existence of subjects who do not conform to the phantasm of normative citizenship. (Muñoz 1999, 4)

Muñoz, however, acknowledges the political insufficiencies and messiness of disidentification, as a way of engaging the contradictory yet productive push-and-pull of political challenge and complicity (5, 9).

---

sociopolitical visibility, where LGBT and LGBT-friendly communities have been gathering at Hong Lim Park in the month of June, since 2009, "to celebrate inclusiveness, diversity and the freedom to love, with the formation of a giant Pink Dot in Speakers' Corner" (http://pinkdot.sg, accessed June 23, 2013). See, particularly, the very touching campaign video, directed by Boo Junfeng, for the June 29, 2013 Pink Dot event: http://pinkdot.sg/pink-dot-2013-drives-the-message-home-with-new-campaign-video/, accessed June 23, 2013. The video presents a form of "homonationalism"—to appropriate Jasbir K. Puar's terminology (Puar 2007)—as part of its tactic of queer visibility, though for a very different agenda from that of Puar's American context. The crafty use of Dick Lee's "Home," the 1998 National Day song, as the video's musical soundtrack, seeks to reclaim Singapore as home on behalf of LGBT Singaporeans, a subtle but incisive critique of how queer illegality has rendered and continues to render them as second-class citizens. For an updated and detailed analysis of LGBT activism in Singapore, including the Pink Dot movement, see Chua (2014).

> Disidentification is about recycling and rethinking encoded meaning. The process of disidentification scrambles and reconstructs the encoded message of a cultural text in a fashion that both exposes the encoded message's universalizing and exclusionary machinations and recircuits its workings to account for, include, and empower minority identities and identifications. (Muñoz 1999, 31)

Yonfan's film confronts the existential burden of Singapore's queer history through its epigraphic framing, but the film then proceeds to scramble and recode political meanings of queer identification and its reactive approach to the ontological challenges posed by homophobia. In other words, the film playfully reroutes the seriousness of Singaporean queer politics not by denying its significance but by rethinking textually alternate modes of representation and relationality in response to this politics.

To accomplish this goal, the film toys with the visuality of queer sex and sexuality on screen through its soft-core aesthetics. The remainder of this chapter seeks to delineate the theoretical contours of this sexual visuality, to tease out filmic details for analytical scrutiny, and to suggest the film's disidentificatory and interventional potentiality in engaging queer Singapore politics, while simultaneously, if not contradictorily, outfitting itself for a global audience's gaze as transnational queer cinema.

Sexual Visuality as Intervention

In *Screening Sex* (the follow-up monograph to her revolutionary study of porn, *Hard Core*), Linda Williams notes that sex on screen, in its various cinematic incarnations, "is not a stable truth that cameras and microphones either 'catch' or don't catch. It is a constructed, mediated, performed act and every revelation is also a concealment that leaves something to the imagination" (Williams

2008, 2). But, even more importantly for our purposes, she identifies the affective capabilities of screen sex, both in alienating "us from the immediate, proximate experience of touching and feeling with our own bodies, while at the same time bringing us back to feelings in these same bodies" (1–2). In addition, "our bodies both take in sensation and then reverse the energy of that reception to move back out to the outside world." Therefore, when it comes to "sexual arousal [that] was once deemed antithetical to all civilized public culture, now, through screening sex, our bodies are not simply shocked into states of arousal but habituated and opened up to this changing environment in newly socialized ways." Cinematically "playing at sex, too, is a way of habituating our bodies to a newly sexualized world in which vicarious forms of sexual pleasure are now on/scene . . . We then begin to see that a variety of responses are possible: shock, embarrassment, arousal, but also, and most important, imaginative play . . . [T]he imagination can play with the most concealed and modest as well as the most revealed and explicit of images and sounds" (18–19). This theoretical conception of sex on screen does not suggest that sex and sexuality, like all textual and filmic inscriptions, are inherently and automatically critical in their politics. Deployment, context, and interpretation help determine their potential for a progressive mode of political critique.

The confluence of Williams's and Muñoz's theoretical ideas allows me to posit screening sex in Yonfan's *Bugis Street* as a disidentificatory reworking of various visual, sonic, and narrative iterations of sexual desires, sexual practices, sexed bodies, gendered sexualities, and sexualized genders. These playful iterations reinsert sex, unabashedly, back into the philosophical and political "seriousness" of queer politics. It strategically messes and dirties up the normalization and mainstreaming of queer relations—the notion that we are just like straight folks in the way we love one another, embrace marital monogamy, and have children like ordinary families, as long as we do not talk about our unsanitary and perverse sexual preferences and practices. In other words, the straight world offers us social inclusivity on the condition that we desexualize our sexual self-representation. The in-your-face sex and sexuality seen on screen must then have a powerful affective and political resonance, especially for a film that is made in and is about a specific geographical site in Singapore. Sexual visuality in *Bugis Street*, thus, ruptures the heteronormative logic I have identified above by resisting the reification of a desexualized homonormativity. The film also dodges strict sexual and gender categorizations by maintaining a libidinal fluidity in its crossing of boundaries and in its rhizomatic couplings and de-couplings.[5] To parse out in concrete cinematic terms the above theoretical abstractions, I offer the accompanying analyses of the film's sexual visuality under the following headings: (1) erotic embodiments, (2) libidinal crossings, (3) narrative subversions, and (4) transgender representation and relationality.

---

5. For the notion of coupling, I am relying on Deleuze and Guattari's formulation of "desiring-machines" in *Anti-Oedipus*: "Desire constantly couples continuous flows and partial objects that are by nature fragmentary and fragmented. Desire causes the current to flow, itself flows in turn, and breaks the flows" (Deleuze and Guattari 1983, 5). In *A Thousand Plateaus*, the rhizome signifies "connection and heterogeneity," "multiplicity," and the notion of "anti-genealogy" (Deleuze and Guattari 1987, 7–11). It "contains lines of segmentarity according to which it is stratified, territorialized, organized, signified, attributed, etc., as well as lines of deterritorialization down which it constantly flees. There is a rupture in the rhizome whenever segmentary lines explode into a line of flight, but the line of flight is part of the rhizome" (Deleuze and Guattari 1987, 9).

Erotic Embodiments

First appearing in the film studies journal *Screen*, now almost four decades ago, Laura Mulvey's classic and provocative essay "Visual Pleasure and Narrative Cinema" initiated a paradigmatic shift in feminist film studies and ignited a firestorm of debate over the idea that, especially in classic Hollywood cinema, "the active power of the erotic look" of the camera gaze is heterosexual male (Mulvey 1992, 28). Feminist and queer film scholars have since challenged Mulvey's thesis by arguing for the varied and shifting, gendered and sexual gazes that cinema as a capitalist commodity is capable of engaging. *Bugis Street*, in its own small way, illustrates this visual modality in its erotic embodiments. For starters, director Yonfan trails and fixes his camera gaze fetishistically on beautiful male bodies, clothed, partially clothed, and completely naked. Subject to that gaze are, in order of their appearance on screen, the American sailor, Lola's boyfriend Meng, the male joggers, Drago's Singapore boyfriend Choi, Lian's schoolboy crush, Linda's boyfriend Singh, and Lola's next boyfriend (at the end of the film) Wah Chai.[6] Except for the case of the American sailor where the camera acts as an omniscient voyeur capturing Lola and him having sex, all the other instances feature overlapping gazes between Lian's and/or one or more of the transgender prostitutes' gazes, and that of the camera/audience. Often, diegetically, the characters invite Lian (and, vicariously, the viewer) to partake in the processes of objectifying

---

6. One of the special features is *Yonfan's MANual*, which is included in Disc 2 of the DVD release of the film. The cover describes the special feature in the following manner: "Those fabulous sexy leading men in Yonfan's movies including footage of Chow Yun-fat, Jacky Cheung, Daniel Wu, Anthony Tang, Nicky Wu, Michael Lam . . . in underwear, bathing suits, and sometimes just their birthday suits" (*Yonfan's MANual*, in *Bugis Street*, dir. Yonfan; perf. Hiep Thi Le, Michael Lam, and David Knight [Hong Kong: Far Sun Film Co. Ltd., 2002], DVD).

these tantalizing male bodies. In Lola's absence, Meng flirts with Lian by narcissistically asking her, "Do you like my body?"[7] The transgender prostitutes Zsa Zsa and Sophie salivate over the male joggers as Sophie proclaims: "Look at their legs, their buttocks!" Drago mentors Lian into sexual womanhood by showing her a bunch of teenage schoolboys in white uniforms and saying: "Today, I'll show you the paradise of budding young creatures. See anyone you like Lian?" And, in the case of Wah Chai, the hailing is direct, when Lola rips off his shirt and utters to Lian: "He's got such a nice body, yes?" What is fascinating about these gazes is they are never static in their (dis)identifications. Are they heterosexual female for Lian and female audiences? Should they be considered gay or gay homoerotic by gay and straight male audiences? (And, yes, straight men do look and admire too.) How does one characterize and differentiate between the gazes of a pre-op and a post-op transsexual? What about a MTF (male-to-female) transgender gaze of one who does not choose sexual reassignment surgery and remains biologically male from the waist down? The rhetorical nature of my questions is obvious: the desires in looking flow, turn,

---

7. All references to the film are taken from the director's uncut version: *Bugis Street*, dir. Yonfan; perf. Hiep Thi Le, Michael Lam, and David Knight (Hong Kong: Far Sun Film Co. Ltd., 2002), DVD. According to the DVD's special feature "Artists' Files" in Disc 1, scriptwriter Fruit Chan "wrote the first draft of the original Bugis Street and is some what [*sic*] changed into Singlish by Mr. Yonfan." For citation of the film's dialogue, I have kept as close as I can to the actual dialogue as uttered by the characters, maintaining especially the integrity of the Singlish moments, instead of relying entirely on the English subtitles. (The subtitles attempt to translate the Singlish sections into Standard English.) Also, where necessary, I offer my own English translations of the Singlish, Malay, Mandarin, and Cantonese words and dialogue, for greater clarity or accuracy; and, in rare instances, I have made very minor adjustments to the subtitles, when I do use them, to ensure spelling, grammatical, punctuation, and syntactical correctness, without changing any of the meanings expressed.

and overlap in ways that rupture what is categorically expected of heteronormative conceptions of the cinematic gaze.

It is also essential to consider the characteristics of male visual embodiment, in other words the object of these gazes. Semi-nudity and full nudity predominate in ways that shock and titillate audiences fortunate enough to watch the film when it was first given a limited theatrical release, or those who now have access to the director's uncut version on DVD. I have chosen here two instances in the film to illustrate my point, beginning with the sequence where Lian and Drago (in the only scene where Drago is in conservative male attire) encounter Drago's semi-nude gardener boyfriend at the hospital grounds after they visited Drago's mother. Drago and Lian have bonded earlier over the question of love and romance, with the more experienced Drago explaining how she[8] prefers "men with muscles, like Hercules, Tarzan, [and] Steve Reeves." Much later, as they continue their conversation while leaving the hospital, they run into Choi watering the outdoor plants with a hose. "Mmmm, have a look," teases Drago, as the camera cuts to a medium shot of a muscular man with his shirt off. He looks up squarely into the camera and smiles right into it. The reverse medium close-up shot shows Drago gripping Lian's shoulders as Drago looks on desirously. I will return to this education about love and desire later in the section "Narrative Subversions." But, for now, I want to focus on what Drago is gazing at: the shot cuts back this time to a medium close-up of Choi, a shot which is held for about eleven seconds; which, in cinematic terms, is an extended period of time (unless it is a Tsai Ming-liang film). The camera is forcing us to linger, and linger, on this object of masculine muscularity. Time

---

8. I refer to the MTF transgender prostitutes as "women" and with female pro-
nouns, for the sake of consistency. The gender identification practices of the
transgender are complex. See Valentine (2007, 24–27) for a detailed discussion of these issues, especially his use of the term "transgender." I deploy the
term broadly to include transsexuals, transvestites, and cross-dressers.

Figure 5   *Bugis Street* (dir. Yonfan, 1995), Drago's boyfriend Choi

seems to stand still, as if one were looking at a famous nude painting or Michelangelo's statue of David, and examining the glistening texture of his tanned skin or the sinewy ripples of his musculature. Bathed in the romantic glow of the tropical sunlight, the character Choi exudes a disarming innocence with his unassuming smile and the reflexive gesture of him scratching his left shoulder with his right hand. The idyllic and (seemingly) uncomplicated sexiness of the character reverberates through visual and tactile pathways. But one must not misread this disarming moment of sexual objectification as intellectually and critically vacuous, as delicious as these eleven seconds might be. It is still a mediated image framed by a complex mode of looking: what is the sexual nature of the gaze when it is seen through the eyes of a post-op transsexual such as Drago, who is accoutered as a man in this specific context? The libidinal ambiguities and crossings, a point I will take up in the next section, complicate this gaze. Lian signals her appreciation of this complexity by looking at Drago looking, and then asking the latter if she were "a lesbian," a question with which Drago has once facetiously confronted Lian, earlier in the film, when they were just getting to know each other. The question is less a serious and more a metonymically playful one, with its "absurdity" relaying the slipperiness of desire and its subject-object dynamic.

The second example of male visual embodiment comes in the form of actor Michael Lam as Lola's boyfriend Meng. Considered as the "sexiest man in Hong Kong" by the author of the actor biographies in the DVD,[9] Lam, in much of the film, parades around in either his character's signature white bikini-style underwear or in the nude. Meng is indisputably an immoral cad, as he hangs around Lola for the money and the gifts she showers on him, and for the fact that he takes complete advantage of Lian when she is at her emotional nadir near the end of the film. But like for Lola and Lian, the film also seduces the audience into a cinematic crush on Meng, precisely on account of his physical beauty. The moments of this bad boy unabashedly posing, reclining, and exerting himself in a bodily fashion are multifarious. But the height of gratuitous sexual imagery on screen comes when the film leads the audience to a voyeuristic view of Meng sitting in a wooden barrel taking a bath. He rises from the tub completely naked as he continues to pour water onto himself with a pail. The camera zooms in for a medium shot of him standing before a mirror while he spews out water like a fountain statue. The deployment of the mirror in the shot serves to undercut symbolically the narcissistic involvement of this character. However, the film is no less complicit in abetting this narcissism with its "shameless" display of Meng's muscular body and frontal nudity. My invocation of *shame* and *gratuitous* filmic nudity is meant here to be counterintuitive in its theoretical force, for I am in no way driven by a prudish disposition or a reactionary

---

9. "Artists' Files," special feature in *Bugis Street* (dir. Yonfan; perf. Hiep Thi Le, Michael Lam, and David Knight [Hong Kong: Far Sun Film Co. Ltd., 2002], DVD). While the veracity of this superlative claim is clearly subject to individualized taste, I read it as a statement of marketing ingenuity—sex sells.

moralism to pass judgment on Yonfan's choices. Rather, I see shame and the gratuitous bodily display on screen here as playful disidentificatory interventions, where the film forces audiences to confront the (queer) politics of shame, in partaking of and indulging in this voyeuristic moment. By addressing the negativity of queer life, Richard Dyer observes how "notions and feelings of immorality, deviance, weakness, illness, inadequacy, *shame*, degeneracy, sordidness, disgust and pathos were all part of the notion of queerdom" and argues that "Queer Theory and politics have sought to reclaim the word queer, not so much to cleanse it of its negative associations as to challenge the assumption that these associations are in fact negative" (Dyer 2002, 6–7; emphasis mine). Ellis Hanson, in counterpoint, rewrites the politics of shame in the following manner:

> There is . . . an inevitable logic of failure built into this deployment of shame, and that failure poses a radical challenge to the shaming pieties of law and order, political unity, and even progressive activism. This failure gives shame its disruptive potential, its edge, though that edge is never easily appropriated for a particular political cause. Gay shame, for example, has rarely been attractive to gay politics, except as a villain. Gay pride can be deployed, and certainly has been, as a shaming technique, a conservative tool for assimilation by which gay people whose conduct is deemed relatively normal or acceptable acquire social benefits at the expense of gay people whose conduct is not. It is largely because of this conservative deployment of shame that [Michael] Warner calls for a queer "ethics of shame," a connectedness to others in a queer context where all are fallen and all are shamed. (Hanson 2009, 136)[10]

---

10. Hanson cites a wonderful passage from Warner's *The Trouble with Normal*, which I find worth repeating here, directly from Warner's text: "Shame is bedrock. Queers can be abusive, insulting, and vile to one another, but because abjection is understood to be the shared condition, they also know

Some who theorize queer shame are more cautious about this reclamation, such as George Chauncey who argues for a more restrained deployment of shame: "To the extent that we can talk about shame as a unitary phenomenon at all, surely we need to attend to its historicity and cultural specificity in any particular context and to recall that its production has always been uneven and its modalities varied" (Chauncey 2009, 279).[11] These various theoretical valences of queer shame help frame *Bugis Street*'s shameless populating of male semi-nudity and frontal nudity on screen, as visible and uncompromising resistances to the social, cultural, ideological, and institutional "Asian" conservatism that seeks to bracket, cordon off, sanitize, suppress, repress, censor, and/or completely erase (queer) sexuality and its material and mediated presence.

Libidinal Crossings

What Michel Foucault has so effectively demonstrated in *The History of Sexuality, Vol. 1* is the institutional proliferation of discursive epistemologies on gender and sexuality (Foucault 1978) to reify the impermeable categories that define sexual identification, representation, and relationality. The Kinsey scale[12] and Sedgwick's conception of the homosocial continuum (Sedgwick 1985, 1–2)

---

how to communicate through such camaraderie a moving and unexpected form of generosity. No one is beneath its reach, not because it prides itself on generosity, but because it prides itself on nothing. The rule is: Get over yourself. Put a wig on before you judge. And the corollary is that you stand to learn most from the people you think are beneath you" (Warner 1999, 35).

11. For a more extended discussion of gay shame, see the essays in Halperin and Traub (2009).

12. See Kinsey, Pomeroy, and Martin (1998). Also, check out the Kinsey Institute online: http://www.iub.edu/~kinsey/research/ak-hhscale.html, accessed June 23, 2013.

have disrupted these categories scientifically and theoretically, in their respective ways, while the rhizomatic figuration of desire from the work of Deleuze and Guattari has enabled one to rethink the multidirectional nature of libidinal flows. It is one thing to grapple with these concepts intellectually, and it is another to come into visual and auditory contact with their cinematic portrayals. Yonfan relies on the shock waves that the rupturing of heteronormative narrative and visual conventions sends—conventions that mainstream cinemas have so habituated us into expecting and accepting. *Bugis Street* multiplies the shock value of these moments through the various iterations of sexual and gender crossings, narrative traps for which the film keeps setting the audience up.

The first soft-core sex scene that I want to focus on to demonstrate this point is the one between Lola and the American sailor, who is on stopover shore leave before being shipped to the Vietnam War. The narrative trajectory of this subplot begins rather traditionally with the sexy sequence of an "Oriental" maiden seducing an American sailor, who is far away from his homeland: the film-noir saxophone soundtrack imbues the mise-en-scène with a heightened sensuality, as cheongsam-clad Lola stands in the shadows of the darkened row of shop-houses and looks smolderingly into the camera, beckoning the entranced sailor like a siren with her pout and the come-hither flick of her finger. The narrative and/or thematic echoes to Hollywood films of the 1950s and 1960s, such as *Love Is a Many-Splendored Thing* (1955), *Sayonara* (1957), and *The World of Suzie Wong* (1960), very quickly and abruptly end here.[13] The fact that even the newly arrived Lian, in her teenage romantic imagination, misreads the Lola-sailor encounter as "a sad departure of an American gentleman and a Chinese girl" that is "so sad, so touching but so lovely . . . like *The World of Suzie Wong*"

---

13. See Gina Marchetti's analysis of the racialized sexuality in these films (Marchetti 1993).

(she tells her pen pal Maria) is testament to Hollywood's impact on the kind of interracial romantic imaginary that prevails the world over.

But where this ideologically hegemonic thematic structure ends, *Bugis Street*'s radical perversion and subversion of it begin with the intense sexuality of the cross-cultural encounter: the inebriated sailor is taken by Lola in a trishaw, in the rain, to Sin Sin Hotel. The close-up shot of the couple making out focuses on him running his hand up through the slit of her dress, caressing her knees and thighs. The long, low-angle shot of the trishaw frantically making its way to the hotel is bathed in sensual blue lighting. Lola imploring the trishaw driver to "be quick" in Cantonese only intensifies the erotic urgency of these racialized sexed bodies in heat. In a series of scenic cuts, the sailor and Lola make out in the hotel lobby and on the edge of the staircase, before entering her bedroom for sex. At one point on the staircase, the camera zooms in, like a porn flick, to a medium close-up of Lola unzipping the sailor's pants ready to go down on him, only to be interrupted by an irate hotel customer shouting from his room: "Oh fuck off! Go and fuck in your own room. Stop making so much noise here. Every night so damn noisy! Make me more horny." This offscreen voice functions as a pornographic preamble to the wild sex that is to be expected in Lola's room, just as the sailor's proclamation of "I'm gonna ride you" denotes the same. Foreplay moves rapidly from Lola's bed, against her dresser, and finally onto the window sill where he has sex with her, with his tight naked ass exposed to the camera—another instance of rear nudity that could fit into my arguments about erotic embodiments.

So far, the narrative moves are still relatively traditional: one based on 1950s and 1960s white male fantasy of available Oriental women in global adventures, and the other on heterosexual (soft-core) pornographic plotlines. But what really turns things around ideologically is the morning-after sequence. Lola examines the sleeping sailor, kisses him on his chest, and turns over the blanket to examine his crotch, all the while whispering to the unconscious man the terrible fate awaiting him in the horror that is the Vietnam War: "You know sailor boy. Just sleep a little bit longer. When your ship reaches Vietnam, you won't get to sleep at all." The irony not only insinuates an anti-colonial and/or postcolonial inflection (vis-à-vis texts like *Eastern Windows* and *Bugis Street Blues*) but it also reverses agency and subjectivity (in counterpoint to James Eckardt's *Singapore Girl*) into the hands of the transgender protagonist. The soldier awakens to anger at the fact that he has had intercourse with a transgender prostitute and that Lola now demands payment for her services. His anger is only constrained by the arrival of Lola's "police," the Chinese triad gangsters, who force him to pay Lola:

Sailor: "Where's my other fucking shoe?!"

Lola: "Damn your fucking shoe. Hey you know what you're playing with. You got me from Bugis Street, alright? I know you're a sailor, good looking and all that, but don't fuck with me. Pay up, pay up!"

Sailor: "Me pay up? You're the one who should pay up. You got what the fuck you wanted . . . And all I got was a fake fucking pussy."

Lola: "You have a lot of fuck in your mouth, don't you? Don't fuck with me. Hey, my pussy is as good as any other and you enjoyed it, OK? You don't pay up I'll call the police."

. . .

(Shot/reverse shot of the sailor stopping at the stairs, and the gangsters and other prostitutes waiting for him at the bottom of the staircase. Lola sashays down the stairs.)

Lola: "They are my police."

(Shot of the gangsters smiling and looking threateningly. Lola smugly cozies up to the sailor from behind.)

Lola: "Do you still want to fuck them? Money please!"

Enriching this postcolonial critique of "Third World" sex tourism that has been part of the Euro-American military R&R and of the international sex trade that has persisted till the present is the cultural anxiety of sexual crossings that have similarly engendered the homosexual panic engulfing the British Royal Navy in the real Bugis Street episode (which I have discussed in Chapter 1). While it is possible that, in his drunken state, he may have misrecognized Lola's "pussy" for the "real" thing, her "pussy" must have felt real enough for him to have such pleasurable sex in the first place. His anger only betrays a hetero-masculinist anxiety for having crossed sexual boundaries with such ease, for he probably knew what he was getting into when he visited Bugis Street in the first place, as Lola reminds him. The nature of Lola's transgenderism is also unclear, a point of particular importance here. Is she a pre-op or post-op transsexual? Or, is she just a gay man dressed as a woman? The lack of certainty matters in terms of the physical nature of their sexual liaison (just as David Henry Hwang's *M. Butterfly* so artfully demonstrates). Did the sailor and Lola have sex in the heterosexual sense, or did they engage in gay anal sex? Is the sailor harboring gay or bisexual tendencies that have now returned from the repressed, which the carnivalesque atmosphere of Bugis Street only so easily elicits? The point I am trying to drive home here is that queer sexuality in this sequence fractures the ideological rectitude of colonial and neo-imperialist heteronormative masculinity (especially as seen in men from the military) with the film's overt sexual visuality.

Another nuance of libidinal crossings that I want to highlight is the productive contradictions springing from the intersection of gender morphologies and sexual practices and identifications. The sequence where transgender prostitutes Zsa Zsa and Sophie ogle and voyeuristically spy on a group of male joggers comes to mind as an instance. The sequence opens with a ground-level close-up of feet running away from the camera with Zsa Zsa's and Sophie's feet appearing in the foreground of the frame. Zsa Zsa exclaims "what a sight!" and Sophie tells her to "[l]ook at their legs, their buttocks!" These expressions of corporeal appreciation are immediately followed by a shot of one of the men patting his buddy's ass as they jog away, a homoerotic gesture that is not lost on Sophie: "Hey! What's he doing, ah?" Here, Sophia Siddique accurately observes how "[t]he stability of the gaze is rendered problematic because the transsexual characters collapse categories of sex and gender; the gaze can no longer be coded as either masculine or feminine" (1999/2000, 85), at least not heteronormatively so. After the men turn around, jog past, and then flirt with Zsa Zsa and Sophie with their looks and waves, the sequence cuts to a series of shots of the men now bathing together in the nude. Using jump cuts to suture about five different shots of the same scene, director Yonfan elliptically prolongs the gaze on these men in a kind of queer cinematic temporality (a theoretical point I will discuss in detail in Chapter 4) that layers the processes of looking at the men in all their naked glory, as they are having a wonderfully homoerotic time pouring water on each other and having wet towel fights. By the time Yonfan gets to the fifth shot, the viewer finally catches a glimpse of full frontal male genitalia, again. This extended gaze on the men is from Zsa Zsa's and Sophie's point of view. A low-angle medium close-up of the women peeking through the glass door also reveals them vicariously simulating sex, with Zsa Zsa kissing Sophie's hand:

Zsa Zsa: "Which one do you like Sophie?"

Sophie: "Please lah. I'm not as cheapskate as you."[14]

14. The expression "lah" functions as an exclamatory remark in Singlish syntax that offers a range of emphatic inflections.

Zsa Zsa: "I love them all . . . Don't forget, right, we promised them to do a lesbian show for free."

Sophie: "I won't do it for free!"

Zsa Zsa: "Please Sophie, please. Just once and for all. Please Sophie."

This homoerotic display is not the only instance in the film for these transgender characters. After Meng returns and has make-up sex with Lola, the group comprising of Maggie, Zsa Zsa, and Sophie leans up against Lola's room door to eavesdrop as they playfully simulate an orgiastic melee that entwines and entraps an utterly confused and mortified Lian. In another scene where Drago is selling her beauty products to the prostitutes in her room, Zsa Zsa and Sophie recline on Drago's bed while Sophie caresses Zsa Zsa's breast, thus incurring Drago's admonition to not be "so obscene" and to "pay attention if you want to be ladies!" (Drago's mock maternal disposition is obvious when we see in the lobby-turned-dance hall scene Lola and Drago sensually dancing very close to each other with lips almost touching; and later on the street, Lola jokes about how they will suddenly "become lesbians" and then plants a light kiss on Drago's lips.) The homoerotic jostling amongst the male joggers intersects the parallel homoerotic performativity of the transgender prostitutes, generating a network of desires that flow and intermingle in unpredictable formations. Again, because we do not know the bodily sexed status of some of these women (an ignorance that advances the political efficacy of the film's tactic), how does one interpret the significance of these multidirectional gazes? Is Zsa Zsa and Sophie's desire for the jogging men gay, heterosexual (in its imaginary), or queer (in its fluidity)? Who are these men performing to in their consciousness of Zsa Zsa's and Sophie's gazes, as they run past them and flirtatiously wave? What does Zsa Zsa's imploring of Sophie to play being "lesbians" signify of Zsa Zsa's relationship to Sophie—displaced sexual energy, gay relationality, lesbian mimicry, or transgender sex that disrupts the heterosexual model? What erotic pleasures will these men derive from this "lesbian show" by transgender individuals, and how are these pleasures accommodated in the compulsory heterosexuality of these men's lives and identities (a question that one can similarly ask of these "straight" sailors who spend their R&R time dipping their toes into the murky waters of Bugis Street)? Not being able to answer these questions is part of the rhetorical point.

To close this section, I want to return to the film's deconstructive potentiality in addressing the philosophical/political binary opposition between mind and body—an essentialist logic that conceives the mind in the idealist terms of philosophical, intellectual, and spiritual transcendence, purity, and superiority; and the body as the poorer material expression of the mind, and hence derivative, corrupted, and unsanitary.[15] My approach here is to frame, self-reflexively, my readings above about overt sex and sexed bodies on screen, and the playful "perversions" that *Bugis Street* deploys, not by politically idealizing these sexual presentations so as to reverse, simplistically, the hierarchical structuring of the mind/body binarism—that is, to argue reductively for sex and nudity on screen as always inherently good or efficacious. Rather, I see the body and the mind as coterminous in their psychical and physiological interdependency and interaction in the holistic construction of subjectivity and identity.[16] *Bugis Street* seems cognizant of the

---

15. One could trace this logic in its different formulations from Plato, the various Judeo-Christian religious traditions, to the more recent contemporary philosophical and psychological theories. For more detailed analysis, I point readers to Elizabeth Grosz's excellent *Volatile Bodies* (Grosz 1994) and the masterful way it tackles some really complicated issues on this matter.

16. "No part of the body is divested of all psychical interest without severe psychical repercussions. Human subjects never simply *have* a body; rather, the body is always necessarily the object and subject of attitudes and judgments. It is psychically invested, never a matter of indifference" (Grosz 1994, 81).

risk it takes in cinematically presenting the "imperfect" and "dirty" body in sexual play. The disidentification processes that the film engages in are (1) deeply mindful of the politically flawed nature of the diegetic spaces that Bugis Street and Sin Sin Hotel embody and the equally flawed sexed bodies inhabiting those spaces, a mindfulness that contends with and folds its complicity into the messy and unsanitary politics of disidentification, which Muñoz has so carefully pointed out. These processes are also (2) deeply revelatory of the "transformative politics and possibilities" of "worldmaking" (Muñoz 1999, 195).

Firstly, let me consider the flawed nature of these sexed bodies and the world they live in: Meng, Lola, Zsa Zsa, Sophie, and all the other denizens of Sin Sin Hotel are humanly imperfect. Hence, it is this humanity, coupled with the film's sexual visuality, that makes *Bugis Street* work as a politically critical and, in Yonfan's characterization, "dangerous movie from Singapore" (Yonfan 1995). Sin Sin Hotel is basically a brothel, and the generally lighthearted and playful atmospherics Yonfan pairs off with momentary doses of brutal reality. A traumatizing example is in the case of the sexual abuse experienced by Linda, when a customer sodomizes her with a pair of chopsticks. This is the same Linda whose earlier confidence functions as a part of her transgender performativity and public self-representation, the very same Linda whose male genitals are being tickled with a feather duster by another male customer, a moment that traumatizes Lian into the shocking realization that all the female prostitutes in the hotel are or were biological males. Yonfan relentlessly forces us to witness Linda's rape by this tattoo-covered customer (who probably belongs to a triad) as a sight of sheer terror. The high angle shot, connoting the overwhelming force at work here, captures the man pushing Linda onto the bed, slapping her, and then shoving the pair of chopsticks into her. The camera zooms in for and sustains a close-up of her horrified face writhing in painful agony, thereby refusing to spare the audience the depth and intensity of her suffering. This difficult shot is followed later by a medium long shot of a disheveled and disillusioned Linda leaning against the entrance to the hotel lobby and smoking a cigarette. Lian slowly approaches her and enquires after her well-being, before lightly touching Linda's back in a tactile attempt to soothe her. Without turning to look at Lian, Linda philosophizes in Singlish: "I don't know! I don't know what's the problem. Why? Why always must be me? Why am I always the unlucky one? It's so difficult to survive. It's enough. It's enough. I got enough already." This cinematic representation of horrific suffering corresponds to real-life traumas experienced by Bugis Street prostitutes, as a 1972 Singapore newspaper article attests. The report describes how transgender prostitutes were forced not only "to pay off secret society 'protectors,'" but they also had "to suffer the scorn of a society more tolerant of female prostitutes than 'queers.'" Some of their clients were also "men who derive sadistic pleasures out of beating them up" (Yeo, Khoo, and Lee 1972, 9). The plight of these prostitutes and the daily dangers they face function as the awful flipside of the political coin, illuminating the conflicted problematics that *Bugis Street* as a disidentification text faces. It is this pairing of play and plight that politically elevates *Bugis Street* above the sexploitative soft-core in Hong Kong cinematic history that is supposedly its genre predecessor.

Secondly, it is crucial to understand the "worldmaking" possibilities that Muñoz talks about and what the concept suggests about *Bugis Street*, nudity, and sex on screen. "The concept of worldmaking delineates the ways in which performances . . . have the ability to establish alternate views of the world. These alternative vistas are more than simply views or perspectives; they are oppositional ideologies that function as critiques of oppressive regimes of 'truth' that subjugate minoritarian people,"

Muñoz explains. "Oppositional counterpublics are enabled by visions, 'worldviews,' that reshape as they deconstruct reality. Such counterpublics are the aftermath of minoritarian performance . . . Disidentificatory performances opt to do more than simply tear down the majoritarian public sphere. They dissemble that sphere of publicity and use its parts to build an alternative reality" (Muñoz 1999, 195–96). The nudity and sex on screen in *Bugis Street* constitute such performances. It reimagines the historical Bugis Street into an alternate cinematic universe that challenges the oppressive media censorship laws, the anti-gay legislation, and the homophobic public spheres in Singapore. Part of the political and epistemological efficacy of the sexed naked body is best summed up, rather poetically, by Giorgio Agamben in his reflections on human nudity: "The naked, simple human body is not displaced here into a higher and nobler reality; instead, liberated from the witchcraft that once separated it from itself, it is as if this body were now able to gain access to its own truth for the first time" (Agamben 2011, 102).

Narrative Subversions: The Heteronormative Coming-of-Age Story Retold

The sexual coming-of-age story of the sixteen-year-old teenager Lian from Melaka[17] is really a "queer" narrative. I am being deliberately provocative here (probably in the same spirit with which Drago asks Lian, "Are you a lesbian?"), though with specific interpretive reasons in mind. Firstly, the sexual coming-of-age story has provided the narrative foundation for numerous mainstream Hollywood films, including *The Graduate* (1967), *Carrie* (1976), *The Blue Lagoon* (1980), *Porky's* (1982), *American Pie* (1999),

---

17. I am abiding by the subtitle usage of Melaka, which is the Malay version of Malacca, a historical tourist town in West Malaysia.

Juno (2007), and, most recently, the delightful *Moonrise Kingdom* (2012). Most of them revolve around heterosexual initiation, or their plot trajectory frequently returns the protagonist, overtly or implicitly, to conservative mainstream understandings of heteronormative romantic love and family relations, after the character experiences certain identity, emotional, psychological, social, and/or physical crisis. While Lian's story in *Bugis Street* is mostly rather conventional in its narrative arc, the points of crisis are resolved in ways that can be read as subversive of genre expectations—rather queerly, I might add. Secondly, the queerness of Bugis Street, Sin Sin Hotel, its transgender occupants, and their clientele and/or lovers provides the spectacular backdrop for the focal plot point of Lian's sexual awakening. The notion that queerness plays second fiddle to and offers a utility role in shoring up heteronormativity is a standard device and trope in mainstream cinematic history.[18] Though this critique of *Bugis Street* (which I have also deployed earlier in my analysis of Koh Buck Song's *Bugis Street: The Novel* in Chapter 1) may to a certain measure be convincing, I do also want to offer a more counterintuitive reading that disturbs the binary labor of the hetero-homo divide, by viewing the relationship between Lian and the community of Sin Sin Hotel as a form of queer pairing or alliance. This connectivity has a palimpsestic quality that incorporates Lian into and, hence, enriches the queer sexual visuality of the film.

The conventional element of Lian's sexual awakening is in her movement from innocent fantasy to corporeal experience. But what is subversive about Lian's sexual education is the unpredictable

---

18. This is clearly changing as more LGBT sexual representations are finding their way onto center stage in not only art-house film productions but also mainstream cinema and television, especially in the United States. For a study of this difficult and fraught history of queer cinematic presence in mostly American films, see *The Celluloid Closet* (Russo 1987), which was made into a fantastic documentary of the same title in 1995.

nature of how it occurs, what she actually learns, and how the libidinal crisis that she encounters as a pubescent teenager is finally resolved. Lian's backstory begins with the classic country-girl-arriving-in-a-big-city motif, which unfortunately imagines Melaka (and metonymically Malaysia) as the less developed backwater of a cosmopolitan and urban Singapore. Affirming this stereotype are Lian's country outfits, her goody-two-shoes haircut, that wide-eyed countenance, and her perpetually (and, to some, cloyingly) cheery disposition. Her notions of sexual relations are grounded in a romanticized amalgamation of Hollywood fantasies and Chinese cultural typologies. Yonfan carefully constructs the framing of her arrival at Sin Sin Hotel to coincide with the departure of the American sailor after the row he had with Lola. In an exterior long shot of the hotel and its main entrance, Lian inconspicuously enters from screen left just as the sailor exits from screen right. The compositional and kinetic symmetry purposefully undercuts the naïve misreading that Lian renders of Lola's relationship to the sailor as a romantic one, a fiction that parallels the cross-cultural love story in *The World of Suzie Wong*. Coloring this misreading is also Lian's own teenage romance that she has experienced in Melaka, a "secret" that she shares with her pen pal Maria (and, hence, with the audience): "The future looks shining brightly for me, but dear Maria, I still miss the simple days I spent in Melaka. I have to tell you the secret. The day I left the house my young master actually cried for me." Much of this romantic fantasy is sustained through the first half of the film. In a sequence where Lian engages in "girl talk" with Lola, Zsa Zsa, Sophie, and Maggie, she confides in them her dreamy projection of this romance: "In Melaka, young master. So young. So handsome. So rich. So many women. But young master only crazy about me. Other maids got jealous. That's why I come here. Do all your dirty laundry and underwear . . . But, when young master come, I will hire all of you to be my maid. And do my dirty laundry and underwear." The class structuration in the Malaysia-Singapore social tension also plays itself out in this fabulation. And, finally, Chinese cultural traditionalism also defines Lian's figuration of the romantic male partner. In the scene where she is cleaning Lola's room near the beginning of the film, Lian uses the feather duster to enact scenes from Chinese opera where she is at one moment a woman warrior and at another the female lover who melodramatically proclaims "I love you! . . . I love you!" There is also the sequence where Drago has a conversation with Lian about love, where the former expounds the desirability of muscled men. Lian shakes her head when Drago asks, "Don't you like muscles?" Her reply is that muscles are "ugly" because she prefers "the romantic, poetic type," an opinion that will evolve for her. But for now, my point here is to identify in "the romantic, poetic type" Lian's reliance on a cultural historical idea of the *wen* masculinity of the Chinese scholar.[19] The country/urban, idyllic innocence/corrupted experience, binary opposition is, in my opinion, the least interesting and most problematic of Lian's narrative. But its presence is understandable in that it functions as a point of "presexual" origination with which to both situate and act as a foil to the oppositional quality of Lian's education and transformation, at the hands of the transgender occupants of Sin Sin Hotel, into the sexual adult that she becomes at the end of the film.

When I label Lian's backstory as "pre-sexual," I am not suggesting that sexuality is absent from her identity and fantasy constructions; but that the materiality of sex in all its "dirtiness"

---

19. According to Kam Louie, the *wen-wu* (文武) balance in Chinese masculinity has evolved through ancient Chinese history: "This *wen-wu* paradigm is particularly relevant to understanding masculinity because it invokes both the authority of the scholar [*wen*] and that of the soldier [*wu*]. Chinese masculinity . . . can be theorised as comprising both *wen* and *wu* so that a scholar is considered to be no less masculine than a soldier. Indeed, at certain points in history the ideal man would be expected to embody a balance of *wen* and *wu*" (Louie 2002, 11).

has been elided, or screened over as cinematic "concealment" (Williams 2008, 2). But Linda Williams's identification of the paradoxical "double meaning of the verb *to screen*" is critical here in that not only have the movies offered Lian a sanitized version of prostitution, as demonstrated in her allusion to *The World of Suzie Wong* (for Lian seems cognizant of what prostitution is when she first arrives in Singapore), but also *Bugis Street* the film functions as a cinematic space of screening sex, the "revelation" (Williams 2008, 2) of sex with which Lian comes face to face diegetically. What she learns in confronting the physical realities of sex at Sin Sin Hotel implodes the heteronormative ideology of gender construction and performativity. For example, in witnessing Linda's male genitals being played with by her male customer, Lian is so traumatically disoriented that she bolts out of the room and throws up over the staircase railings, an extreme reaction that solicits not sympathy but ridicule from Zsa Zsa, Sophie, and Maggie, who happened to be passing by:

> *Zsa Zsa*: "What is going on here?"
>
> *Maggie* (in Mandarin): "Lian, what are you doing? What is it?"
>
> *Lian*: "Linda . . . " (She points in the direction of Linda's room.)
>
> *Sophie*: "What about Linda?"
>
> *Lian*: "She . . . she's a man!"
>
> (The women break out into hysterical laughter.)
>
> *Maggie* (in Mandarin): "Oh dear, she's a man? I am a man too."

Maggie mischievously exposes her breasts to Lian and shakes them in front of her. Lian runs off in horror, while Sophie calls Lian a *sua gu* (山龜), which means literally "mountain tortoise" in the Chinese dialects of Hokkien and Teochew, thereby denoting Lian's lack of urban sophistication and understanding.

It is easy to judge harshly the transgender prostitutes' naughty

responses to Lian's discombobulation, but I want to rethink the
insensitive humor as part of a campy excess that is routed through a
circuitry of queer shame and the queer ethics that Michael Warner
talks about. The ethics of queerness flows from the transgender
prostitutes having been shamed before, laughing at the shock
response that others find in seeing their transgender bodies,
amusing themselves with the shamelessness of their outrageous
play, to arriving at an affective commiseration with their Other as
a fellow human being. Lola is the first one to run after Lian when
the latter decides to return to Melaka: "Don't go. You have to
forgive them. You know some people are not the same as others.
And I promise they're harmless. Come back with me please!" Lola's
invocation of human differences as the common denominator that
unites us is a powerful one, for it teaches Lian (and the viewer)
the queer ethics of acceptance. Lola then holds Lian by the hand
and leads her back to the hotel, an affective move that mobilizes
touch as part of human comfort and connectivity. The success of
this affectivity Lola cements when she tells Lian at the threshold
of the hotel entrance, "You'll like this place. This is my home and it
will be your home too." The scene immediately following this one
features the previously breast-shaking Maggie now reaching out
to Lian, which perfectly instantiates the circuitry of queer ethics:
"*Mei Mei* (妹妹 meaning "younger sister" as a term of endearment
in Mandarin), don't be upset. I frightened you yesterday, didn't
I? . . . Sometimes people like us overdo it. Don't be angry." Maggie
then presents Lian with a beautifully wrapped gift, which Lian
claims to Maria that she will "treasure it always" because she "was
so touched and it was so beautiful that . . . [she] never wanted to
open it."

After her return to Sin Sin Hotel, Lian bonds with the
transgender prostitutes as sisters and is particularly close to Drago
and Lola. The prostitutes treat her like one of their own and they
share secrets with one another. Interestingly, like sisters, they are

also present when Lian has her first menstruation, which is a female rite of passage into sexual adulthood and embodiment. Yonfan's choice of including such a seemingly gratuitous and unusual scene is pregnant with queer possibilities. According to Lauren Rosewarne, menstruation on screen constitutes "rare occasions when producers dared eschew the popular taboo and allowed women to do *on* screen what they so frequently do *off* screen" (Rosewarne 2012, 2). In the case of a girl's first period, or menarche, "menstruation is celebrated not just as a generic developmental milestone, but one with *life-giving* properties; the girl is being welcomed into a community of those who can procreate, notably by the woman who gave her life" (42). Rosewarne also isolates the heterosexual valences of menarche, which is "presented on screen as the instigator for adult, romantic feelings" and "the social expectations of heterosexual performance" (59–60). Lian's reaction to the sudden and, to her, inexplicable blood flow comports with the standard representations in screen history: Lian hysterically cries out, "I am bleeding . . . I am dying," characterizing how "menarche [is often] interpreted as impending death" (Rosewarne 2012, 50) or as a source of "humiliation" (49). In what sense then can this scene of Lian's menarche be construed queerly, apart from the fact that it fits into the spectacle of the film's sexual visualities—in this case, the physical manifestation of female corporeality—and that it nestles appropriately into the plot structure of the sexual coming-of-age genre? Does not Lian's menstrual flow visually mark her biologically "authentic" femininity, vis-à-vis the MTF transgender individuals surrounding her, hence winnowing the "real" from the "fake"?[20] The queerness I want to argue for here lies in the relational enabling that transgenderism plays in Lian's budding sexuality.

20. Rosewarne helpfully references the work of Chris Bobel who points out that "some preoperative transmen do menstruate (as do many intersexuals)" (quoted in Rosewarne 2012, 5; endnote 3). See also Bobel 2010.

Instead of having maternal support and celebration of menarche (in accordance with the heteronormative pattern that Rosewarne has discerned in pop cultural representations), Lian is surrounded by her transgender sisters when her period arrives. The traumatic fight that broke out between Drago and the others may have physiologically precipitated her menstrual flow. This contiguous relationality is further punctuated when these women come to her aid by lifting her off the floor and onto Drago's bed, while screaming for Mrs. Hwee, the hotel manager, to come help. After smelling a dab of Lian's menstrual blood, Mrs. Hwee proclaims in Singlish, "Aiyo, Ah Lian, your big auntie has just arrived today lah!"[21] Diegetically, the biologically female Mrs. Hwee—the film, queerly, does not confirm or deny this assumption—is a stand-in for the maternal figure in this context, but the additional queer twist in this case is a meta-filmic one: the character is played by Gerald Chen in drag.

Lian's sexual education is complete when the transgender community teaches her the feminist lessons of (1) gender performativity and its empowering possibilities, and (2) the embracing of female sexual desires that do not necessarily conform to normative expectations of respectable heterosexual romance. In the first instance, the women at Sin Sin Hotel, one evening, temporarily transform Lian from a dowdy domestic worker to an honorary "prostitute," whom they christen as the "Snow White of Bugis Street"! Following the makeover conventions in reality television shows, Yonfan constructs a before-and-after sequence where Lian, with her back to the camera, is first being subjected to a makeover carousel—a humorous series of jump cuts where Lola, Zsa Zsa, Sophie, and Drago each take turns to assist her with

---

21. Like "lah," "aiyo" has a similar exclamatory usage, although its inflection is incredulity, surprise, or even mild derision. "Big auntie" is a Singaporean metaphor for menstruation.

makeup, dress, and hairstyle. Drago then presents Lian to a lobby full of cheering sailors and hotel clients, as if it were the latter's debutante ball. Lian's costume is ironically contrary to her Snow White moniker in that she is accoutered in a leathery corset and knee-high faux leather boots, an S/M outfit in which Dr. Frank-N-Furter (Tim Curry) of *The Rocky Horror Picture Show* (1975) will find himself very comfortable.[22] The sisters continue Lian's initiation into the world of Bugis Street by teaching her how to sashay when they make their way to their destination. A fight breaks out as one of the non-Sin Sin Hotel prostitutes accuses Lian of encroaching on her turf. The sisters spring to Lian's defense and, like all good sisters, they fight off the accuser, enabling Lian to make a run for it. Lian's "very confusing" night does not end there. Instead, she runs into the rogue Meng when Mrs. Hwee asks her to change the light bulb, again, in Lola's room. This time, in contradistinction to the first light bulb-changing scene, Lian is no longer the timid and frightened wallflower in face of Meng's aggressive seduction. She seems empowered by her new persona and outfit, which has turned Meng on further. She orders Meng around, uses his body to step off the chest after changing the bulb, slaps him when Meng moves in for a kiss, and smirks dismissively in erotic play, before leaving Meng sexually unfulfilled and hankering for more. In the context of fat studies, Michael Moon argues that the fat transvestite diva, such as John Waters's Divine, embodies "a certain interface between abjection and defiance . . . This combination of abjection and defiance often produces a divinity-effect in the subject, a compelling belief that one is a god or a vehicle of divinity" (Moon and Sedgwick 2001, 295).

Of course, Lian is far from fat and is in no manner a transvestite, but Moon's divinity-effect explains her behavior: the outfit she

---

22. Yonfan's fascination with sadomasochistic bondage gear makes a significant re-appearance in his later film *Color Blossoms*.

has on is so out of character for her that she is for all intent and purposes in drag, so to speak. The honorary drag persona allows her to experience queer abjection and to express divine defiance. This divine sense of female empowerment that dress and makeup offer is not lost at all on Lian. As the evening finally comes to a close, she sits in front of her dresser to remove her wig, false eyelashes, and makeup in slow contemplation: "And now, I know the rewards of makeup and the price I have to pay. It gives me courage to do things I've never done before. Somehow, after taking off that mask, I am never the same simple girl anymore. How strange it is to be mature, and how wonderful it is to experience new things. But sometimes, later at night, there are still moments when I long for the sunny breezy days in Melaka. They seem so far away now!" Lian's ambivalence in having entered sexual womanhood is countered by her realization that the gender performativity of makeup and dress is identity transforming as corporeal attachments and extensions; and that this transformation has irrevocably marked her experientially, for good or bad.

The second lesson of embracing her shifting desires and her sexuality as a woman begins when both Drago and Lola converse with Lian about the contradictions of love. After regaling Lian with the aesthetic desirability of muscular men, Drago confides in Lian her experience of first love: "When I was sixteen, I fell in love, in love not with a muscle man, but with an old man. To me, it was love. To him, he wasn't sure that a younger person could love an older person. He said, 'Go back and think about it!' So, I went back and thought about it, and I came back and I said, 'I love you!' And after two months, he dumped me. That much for love. And that much for older balding men." Despite her negative experience, Drago still extols the wonders of being in love: "When you're in love, it's like a butterfly flying non-stop in your tummy . . . [I]t's not everyday you get that feeling." Lola offers a similar tale of love disrupted when she describes her relationship with Meng:

My darkest secret? . . . I hate Meng! I hate him so much I'm so happy he's not around! Yes! He lies to me. He cheats me. Sometimes he beats me, yeah. He even goes off with other women. I'm not stupid . . . I picked him up when I was eighteen at Bugis Street. I was such a flower then. Everyone wanted me. You know there was this rich gentleman from Switzerland who wanted to marry me. Yes! I would be living in his big house with lots of servants. I'd be so grand. [Her happy face turns bitter and sad.] Not only did I give up everything for Meng, I even educated him. Yeah! I taught him the finer things in life. Everything he wears I bought him. I bought him jewelry, I paid his bills, I paid his gambling debts . . . I hate him! . . . [She is near tears.] I hate him so much I'm so happy he's not around . . . [She cries.] I miss him so much.

A physical manifestation of Lola's conflicted feelings of love is Meng suddenly appearing in the room immediately after her speech and the other women leaving the couple to have passionate makeup sex. The personal tales of Lola and Drago disabuse Lian of her fantasies of idealized romance by teaching her that love can be unpredictable, cruel, complicated, and compromised (though they do not dismiss the political usefulness of fantasy, a point I will return to in Chapter 4).

Lian learns this lesson not just vicariously but also personally when she makes certain life choices that subvert the coming-of-age narrative in a powerful fashion. After Drago leaves Sin Sin Hotel immediately following her mother's passing, Lian's sadness is unexpectedly compounded by the arrival of Man Kit, the young master from Melaka that Lian has talked about. With the disillusionment that Lian has been experiencing, one would have assumed, from a narrative standpoint, that Lian's reunion with her first crush will be the conventional, if not convenient, choice she would make. Despite expressing her positive affections for him, that she misses him, Lian insists that Man Kit "go home [and] . . . don't come back!" Her melancholy deepens when nothing comes of her crush on the Singaporean schoolboy—he is completely oblivious of her presence when he and his friends board the bus that Lian is on as she is traveling back to the hotel after seeing Man Kit off. She eventually ends up in the arms of the incorrigible Meng, losing her virginity to him only to find herself abandoned when he leaves Sin Sin Hotel for good after sleeping with her. "I created a fantasy world of my own. But now I realized the only real thing that exists for me is the one person I detest, and even he's gone," Lian confides in Maria. But the film ends in a positive and surprisingly cheery note with Lian regaining her felicitous disposition once more, precisely because her adventure into the realm of the senses, of sexual adulthood, is one that is human life: fecund, unexpected, and layered in all its rich contradictions. The (sexual) choices that she makes involve risks, responsibilities, and repercussions, but they are hers to make, and to own.

Transgender Representation and Relationality

In their book on the history of Singapore film, Jan Uhde and Yvonne Ng Uhde engage what they deem to be the representational flaws of *Bugis Street*. "Underneath the slick surface, the portrayal of the lives of the cross-dressing prostitutes on Bugis Street leaves much to be desired," they contend. "The film might have had the potential to reveal a touchy facet of reality in Singapore had it not been content with being overly exploitative, a weakness which fails to do justice to the sensitive performances of the cast, which included real life transvestites and transsexuals" (Uhde and Uhde 2010, 77).[23] While I share Jan Uhde and Yvonne Ng Uhde's liberal

---

23. The transsexual actors revealed that they "were exploited." Maggie "wanted to act in Bugis Street because [she] . . . thought it would give [her] . . . a chance to do something for [her] . . . 'sisters,'" only to discover that "the plot was insubstantial and [their] . . . roles were shallow." She also points out that

sensibilities toward transgender communities and the oppressed status that the transgender occupy as multiply minoritized citizens in Singapore, I find their political imposition of a sociological/ anthropological expectation of realistic representation problematic. Or, as Helen Hok-Sze Leung puts it, "strong audience investment in 'realistic representation' and 'positive image' often places an undue burden on both queer and transgender characters to be positively representative of whole communities" (Leung 2012, 184). The production of politically and critically effective filmic representations of transgenderism need not be mutually exclusive from the aesthetic excess or artistic license that directors can take. What Uhde and Uhde construe as "overly exploitative," I see as densely playful, ironically excessive, and productively oppositional modes of sexual visualities, a point with which I began this chapter. Some of the best art and art cinema one has seen eschew conventional realism in order to better convey the *realities* of subject formation and characterizations. Furthermore, cinematic realism is subjective, for what is constitutive of realistic representation is funneled through culturally, socially, and politically inflected gazes. Leung correctly observes that transgender "expressions do not result primarily from their self-identification. Rather, they are stand-ins for some notion of 'difference,' whether construed as villainous monstrosity or sacrificial obsession. They sustain a fantasy through which audiences can channel their own anxiety or fascination. When we look at these characters, we are looking at everything *but* transgender subjects, who are nowhere to be found amongst the monsters, victims, and ghosts" (Leung 2012, 189–90).

"[t]he audience may be misled into thinking there is no depth in [their] . . . lives" (quoted in Koh 1995, 24). Katy Yew, the film's producer, disagrees with this perception by arguing that the film "did not intentionally exploit the transsexuals and transvestites" (Koh 1995, 24). The goal was, according to Yew, "to create an awareness of transsexuals and transvestites and what they had to face" (quoted in Koh 1995, 24).

The relaying of transgender subjectivity in *Bugis Street* may not be perfect, but it is in its imperfection that the human flaws and frailties of its subjects are communicated. The film's campy playfulness may spectacularize transgender objectification in conventionally problematic ways, but it is this same playfulness that mobilizes a self-awareness that engages a queer ethics to disrupt self-righteous, judgmental attitudes. To exemplify what I am arguing here, I want to turn to two sequences in the film, one of which involves Lola videotaping Sophie, Zsa Zsa, and Maggie in a home-video confessional, as these women divulge their secrets directly into the camera, in ways that are unexpectedly humorous (dark though they may be) and subjectively sensitive:

> *Sophie*: "I've one secret to tell you girls about sex change. [She snips a tiny pair of scissors as she says this.] After my sex change, the next morning I woke up. Suddenly, I realized my cock's gone. Oh my god, and I shout, 'Doctor, where's my cock? I want my cock back.' The doctor said, 'No, no, no, your cock is gone, gone forever lah! I have one good news to tell you. You gonna have sex everyday for the next six months to keep your vagina hole open!' And the most boring is I had a rubber equipment. Aiyo, it's so long, seven inch. Aiyo, can throw it away. Insert in and out. Throw better lah. And my boyfriend all the time had sex! Aiyo. Then I discover a place, here, right here, paradise of Bugis Street! Yes! Oh, can earn a lot of money. Have sex a lot of men every night. Every night! Oh so good, so lovely. And then I realized, I'm still a good girl. I was told by a doctor to do so."

> (The camera cuts to Zsa Zsa.)

> *Zsa Zsa*: "Now, I want to tell you my darkest secret. I want to be a queen of the queens. And everybody dreams to be a queen. To be a beauty pageant queen. To be a movie queen. And to get married prince, to be a real queen. It's not easy to be a queen. You can't leave home without makeup and let men see your ugly face. You got to put a lot of jewelry. See like mine? It's fake one and nobody

knows. Every year I join beauty contest in Bugis Street. And every year I lose. I fed up to join beauty contest. But trust me, one day I'll be a queen of Bugis Street. And I'll be a queen of the queens."

(The camera cuts to Maggie laughing hysterically.)

Maggie (speaking in Mandarin): "I've always admired Sophia Loren's big tits. So I started to save up so that I could have a pair of big tits like hers. I went to the doctor. I ordered the biggest pair of tits they have. After I returned home, my friends saw me, and they said what beautiful papayas you got there. Then they said shall we play mahjong? Alright, so we started playing mahjong. We played and played, and I was totally excited. Then suddenly I heard 'Bam'! My breast had collapsed! And my white dress turned red. I looked at it and my god! And the next day, I went to the doctor to have it fixed. But this time I didn't want it big. I wanted small ones."[24]

Sophie reflects upon the loss of her penis as part of the trauma of body modification, a physical-psychological expression that undercuts the gender inversion logic of older theories regarding transsexuality. Zsa Zsa brings awareness about the daily difficulties makeup creates in the construction of gender embodiment for the transgender set. And, Maggie highlights with self-deprecating levity the role breasts play in the reification of feminine beauty and sexual worth. Through the personal unveiling of their anxieties about their bodies, these women let the audience in on not only a glimpse of the complex relations between sexual corporeality and transgender subjectivity, but also on how shameless play becomes, for them, a tactic of resistance against and a strategy of survival within a homophobic and often unforgiving world.

My second example of transgender subjectivity and performativity (and the final point of analysis in this chapter) lies in the scenes involving Drago's hospital trips to visit her dying

---

24. Again, for Sophie and Zsa Zsa, I have retained the odd syntax of Singlish throughout their monologues.

mother. These parallel sequences are clearly meant for contrast in the kind of gender performativity that clothing enables. In the first visit to the hospital, Drago is dressed like Wonder Woman in black. Her over-the-top speech and behavioral patterns are also modeled after the female diva, with photos taken with the hospital staff as "fans," and autograph offers that are hilariously rebuffed. "Each time when I come and visit you, they want to take pictures with me It makes me feel like a movie star," proclaims Drago to her mother. During the second visit, Drago comes dressed in conservative male attire, with Lian in tow. Drago's vocal and bodily gestures assume a masculine guise:

> *Mother*: "What happened to you? You dressed like a man!"
>
> *Drago*: "But I am a man, or I was a man! Meet my fiancée Lian. This time it's a real girl!"
>
> *Lian*: "How many fiancées have you had?"
>
> *Drago*: "The kind of fiancée you want to get married to, and have children!"
>
> *Mother*: "Don't tease me! After so many years, I got used to having a daughter. And now I have you back as a son! I'm confused."
>
> *Drago*: "Don't be!"

Drago's gender performance is much more subdued as a man, but no less outrageous in its border crossing. As a post-op MTF transsexual, Drago is (or was) a man and is also a woman—trans-ing as a gender politics of both categorical refusal and acceptance. Another possible interpretation in Drago's choice of performing masculinity is not to read it as a cruel gesture, but to view it instead as a generous and loving one of cultural relationality: s/he is being the good Chinese daughter/son to her/his mother, all at once. I see this interpretive move as an instance of what Helen Hok-Sze Leung deems to be a "different critical strategy" that "focuses on the transing of relational bonds: the ways in which the crossings of gender realign desire, affection, and affinity between people, in a manner that is unpredictable within hetero or homonormative narratives" (Leung 2012, 190). Drago is using her transgender subjectivity to be all that she can be, relationally, to her mother. Lian's voiceover tribute encapsulates the depth of a mother's love that does not simply transcend but fully embraces the trans in the transgender that is Drago: "To bring up a child born as a daughter but embodied as a son. What courage it takes to break all the traditional values. It takes a lifetime to fight. And now she's tired."

In this chapter, I have delineated the contours of *Bugis Street*'s sexual visualities in order to articulate the complex nature of the film's queer and transgender politics: its disidentificatory successes and flaws, as they inhabit the heteronormative zones of Singapore's social conservatism and its antiquated anti-gay penal system. As a transnational queer film, *Bugis Street* should be celebrated for its resistance against the restrictive constraints of Singapore's media culture and its censorship laws. To provide a fair counterbalance, it is also important to acknowledge that the trans in transgender is complicit in enabling the trans in transnational[25]—*Bugis Street* as transnational queer cinema relies on the spectacle of transgenderism to market itself in the art-house cinematic circuits. But, to accept the film's complicity in global cinema's neoliberal politics of capitalist consumerism is in no way an outright disavowal of its political potentiality. For the trans in transnational can be double edged, in that queerness and transgenderism have been

---

25. Song Hwee Lim's essay "Is the Trans-in Transnational the Trans-in Transgender" provides the inspiration for the theoretical intersections between the two terms (Lim 2007). See also David Valentine's ethnographic study *Imagining Transgender*, where he asks how "[t]he intensification of inequalities that have attended neoliberal regimes in the United States and globally" have had an impact on "the politics of transgender" (Valentine 2007, 18).

known to ride the flows of the transnational into the international arena, in seeking recognition of queer existences and the human rights attention they deserve.

4

Bugis Street as Queer Space and Time

Queering Cinematic Space and Time

The official English title of the first volume of director Yonfan's Chinese-language memoir is *Intermission*, but the Chinese title is 楊凡時間, translated as "Yonfan time." This apparent discrepancy between the two versions of the title Yonfan resolves by furnishing his readers with a personal anecdote about his ability to socialize and his desire to be in the spotlight even when he was a student in junior high. The scene he sets for us is the lobby of the Hong Kong City Hall, which was the cultural center in the 1960s and 1970s. During the intermission time of theatrical or musical performances, audiences would gather in the lobby area to mingle and talk about the show. Traipsing amongst the cultural elite is the young Yonfan, who was "an offbeat young person, dressed in a weird fashion, mimicking the lost brother of the dancing group in Jacques Demy's film *The Young Girls of Rochefort*." The teenager, with aspirations for fame, "used the intermission time to wander around and to be a social butterfly in order to get everyone's attention" (Yonfan 2012, 70–71). Yonfan imbues this seemingly mundane social practice with aesthetical and temporal significance. An intermission is a moment of temporal suspension in the midst of the linear progression of an artistic performance. But for Yonfan, it is also a time for social connectivity and for immersing in the artistic and cultural ambience. This seemingly superficial and trivial interval space is really his special time, a Yonfan kind of time. Culturally meaningful time does not stop during these intermissions, but it continues to revolve and fold in on itself in meaningful ways. The metaphoric quality of intermission/Yonfan time translates effectively into the director's reflections about memory and sentimental attachments to people he knows, to the friends he loves, and to the events he sees as momentous in his life. "People and events are not in photos but only in my memories. They just disappear in the flowing of time," muses Yonfan nostalgically (xxvi). The memoir provides him the opportunity to suspend and revisit these points of Yonfan time, allowing him and his readers to immerse in and (re-)experience these moments. I want to argue further that this sensitivity toward time and its meaningful intermissions—the disruption of homogenous time by gaps of reconfigured time that accommodates affectation, relationality, fantasy, and, even, utopian futurity—inflects the way Yonfan constructs his memoir and his films for critically productive purposes.

When the heteronormative ordering of time and space bears down upon sexual minorities, many of them turn to the reimagined temporalities and their spatial projections to fantasize and hope for an alternate universe of liberal acceptance. These imaginings often materialize into various cultural texts, including cinema. Hence, in my consideration of *Bugis Street* as a text of transnational queer cinema, I find it necessary to think about the film's reformulation of the historical and discursive Bugis Street into a cinematic version of queer fantasy and intervention. Thus, the spatial structuration and temporal crossings of the film call out for such critical analysis, which I believe further enriches the already dense layering I have suggested in the archival fabulations and the queer oppositional politics discussed in Chapters 1 and 3 respectively.

The fact that *Bugis Street* is based, however loosely, on a real geographical space in a period of real historical time in Singapore (and that it is a part of the discursive textual network which formulates and fabulates "Bugis Street" as a cultural, political, and aesthetic phenomenon) inherently posits the film's queering of cinematic space and time, especially as the film confronts the ideological consequences of Bugis Street's erasure from Singapore's geographical present and its ultimate relegation to the nation's historical past. In my reading, Yonfan seems conscious enough of this context to inscribe in the film itself the temporal and spatial contiguities between the "real" pro-filmic phenomenon of Bugis Street and the aestheticized and fantastical tracings of *Bugis Street* the film. Signaling the merging of historical reality and cinematic fantasy, the credit sequence, for example, designates "Hiep Thi Le and Residents . . . of Sin Sin Hotel" as the stars of *Bugis Street*, confirming Jan Uhde and Yvonne Ng Uhde's observation that the transgender characters are played by "real life transvestites and transsexuals" (Uhde and Uhde 2010, 77). The "trans" in transgender here could be thought of as invoking the notions of transmission, transition, and transformation, as the film shifts gears diegetically and non-diegetically through time and space. This crisscrossing of fact and fiction is only one in a series of maneuvers that the film makes in its configuration of a queer cinematic time and space, which I unpack in the follow-up sections of this chapter.

Before I begin, it is necessary to offer some theoretical clarification of queer space and time, upon which I rely on Judith Halberstam for assistance:

> A "queer" adjustment in the way in which we think about time,
> in fact, requires and produces new conceptions of space . . .
> "Queer time" is a term for those specific models of temporality
> that emerge within postmodernism once one leaves the temporal
> frames of bourgeois reproduction and family, longevity, risk/
> safety, and inheritance. "Queer space" refers to the place-making
> practices within postmodernism in which queer people engage
> and it also describes the new understandings of space enabled by
> the production of queer counterpublics. (Halberstam 2005, 6)

In other words, queer space furnishes queer subjects with an
alternative social, cultural, and political materiality within the
heteronormative public spheres of geographical, architectural,
and communal existence. To reimagine such queer spaces, like in
the case of *Bugis Street*, cinematic spatiality expands, contracts,
contorts, inscribes, and revises in ways that enable a queer, nostalgic
re-inhabitation of a space previously hijacked; and/or in ways that
retool virtualized spaces for "worldmaking" (Rodowick 2007, 54)
efforts, to forge a queer futurity. In a similar fashion, queer time
questions heterosexual life narrations and, as Elizabeth Freeman
puts it, "[q]ueer temporalities . . . are points of resistance to this
temporal order that, in turn, propose other possibilities for living in
relation to indeterminately past, present, and future others: that is,
of living historically" (Freeman 2010, xxii). Freeman speaks of how
"'queer time' appears haunted" or "elongates and twists chronology"
(Freeman 2010, x) as queer cinematic time unreels itself. It speeds
up, slows down, stands still, flips backward, and/or springs forward
to capture queer loss, queer hope, and/or queer imaginings. In
my discussions of queer cinematic space and time, it is difficult
to disentangle the two concepts because visual representations of
time can only occur in spatial terms, in the same way that space
can only unfold in cinematic time.[1] Thus, my discussion of the film

---

1. "Like photography, film transcribes before it represents while producing

will abide instead by a thematic flow, with analysis of space-time interactions embedded in the process.

Bugis Street as Heterotopia

According to Michel Foucault, heterotopias "are something like counter-sites, a kind of effectively enacted utopia in which the real sites, all the other real sites that can be found within the culture, are simultaneously represented, contested, and inverted. Places of this kind are outside of all places, even though it may be possible to indicate their location in reality" (Foucault 1986, 24).[2] Foucault classifies the brothel as an instance of "extreme types of heterotopia" (27). While not technically a brothel in a conventionally architectural sense, Bugis Street was part of a network of streets that allowed biologically female and MTF transgender prostitutes to ply their wares. Thus, Bugis Street was heterotopic in the extreme sense that Foucault has delineated. Another way of thinking about Bugis Street and the surrounding prostitution district as heterotopic is to consider its liminal presence at the boundaries between Singapore's

---

images in and as movement. As such, films compound the temporal sense of photographs such that what is visible or perceptible in the image is not fixable as a spatial relation in a conventional sense. It is, rather, a movement disjoined from space, which psychologically moves the viewer as the double pursuit of an image both lost to time past and passing in time present. In both photography and film, the virtual is always overrunning the actual: on one hand, there is the hallucinatory projection of events lost to the (virtual) past in the present image; on the other, the irreversible succession of passing presents where space in movement appears and disappears into the virtual time of memory" (Rodowick 2007, 78–79).

2.   In discussing the beginnings of cinematic technology, Mary Ann Doane invokes Foucault's concept to argue that "[t]he 'kinetoscope of time' constitutes . . . both a heterotopia and a heterochrony, offering its spectator an immersion in *other* spaces and times, with the assurance of a safe return to his or her own" (Doane 2002, 3).

urban center and the underdeveloped spaces of the island. I see this liminal ghostly status of prostitution spaces as contesting and inverting, to use Foucault's terminology, the moral respectability of mainstream society, with the queer Bugis Street being doubly heterotopic in this sense.

The "cleansing" and, hence, erasure of Bugis Street was part of the state's urban redevelopment and public housing plans. As Singapore's Housing Development Board began building cheap public housing stretching from the Bugis Street area outwards into the outlying spaces like a fan, the southern city center was similarly subjected to urban modernization that spatially and architecturally kept pace with the government's plans to transform Singapore into the global capitalist city that it is today. The public housing scheme, according to sociologist Chua Beng-Huat, was "used to shore up the family institution, which the government has ideologically adopted formally as the 'fundamental' institution of society" (Chua 1997, 141).[3] The slightly more liberalized city center, which catered to the Western expatriate set, is bounded geographically to create binary spaces, an (unsuccessful) attempt at shielding Singaporeans from the corruptive influences of Western social and cultural practices (or at least a politically strategic display, on the part of the state, in privileging cultural conservatism). Bugis Street, therefore, was too abject in its sexual flagrancy and alterity to coexist with these geographical spheres, even in its liminal state of existence. It had

3. Chua explains the heteronormative familial inflection of the scheme: "Public housing is only available to households. Single people who it is presumed will never marry—males over 45 years old and females of over 40—are eligible to rent, but only then if they share with another person. However, the rules have been relaxed in the early 1990s to allow single people of 35 years and over to purchase 3-room flats at locations outside the central area. Young single people are completely excluded from the equation on the grounds that making public housing available to them would prematurely break up family units" (Chua 1997, 141).

to be scrubbed clean, if not completely erased, for it to fit into the ideological matrix of Singapore's spatial configuration.

As I have pointed out earlier, Bugis Street still exists in Singapore's national imaginary as a queer space. It has become heterotopic in its queer iconicity, despite the cultural anxieties that surround it. It is in this historical context that I want to think of Bugis Street as symbolic or symptomatic of queer space and time. Queer spaces in Singapore were then haunted or haunting spaces. Growing up in the 1980s as a gay teenager, in a post-Bugis Street era, I have vague recollections of how gay and lesbian spaces were ghostly in their social presence. We spoke then in hush tones amongst gay friends about possible locales to meet, one of which is the Hangar, located on Upper East Coast Road that was turned into a gay disco on select days. Roy Tan confirms my own tenuous memory of the space and its spectral existence:

> It was not easy to locate as there were no prominent surrounding landmarks. It was situated within The Summit Hotel . . . [which] was a linear, angular series of single-storey whitewashed buildings, which one could only access by trudging along a length of unpaved road, up a slope leading to the top of a gentle hill . . . The Hangar gradually attracted a clientele of gay men, especially on Sunday nights starting from the early 1980s. Here, they could dance with each other and were not prevented from doing so by the bouncers. Sundays were relatively quiet nights when heterosexuals, who had to work the following Monday, were not so inclined to spend late nights, so this was a lacuna which the management of these establishments and the gay community were eager to fill. (Tan 2012, 137–38)

My anecdotal point, with the aid of Tan's excellent historical archeology, is to underline the critical need for queer spaces in Singapore (from the 1960s to the 1990s, at least) to be conceptualized politically in heterotopic terms.

The cinematic imagining of Bugis Street in Yonfan's film is also heterotopic in its configuration. The central spatial locus is Sin Sin Hotel, which is presented to the viewer as an architectural and communal extension of Bugis Street. (The depiction of the hotel is historically inaccurate. For, according to Roy Tan, "[t]here were no brothels located along Bugis Street itself or the adjoining lanes, as romantically depicted in the movie" (Tan, "Bugis Street: Transgender Aspects). Sin Sin Hotel is, therefore, part of Yonfan and the scriptwriters' fabulation[4]). Bugis Street, as conceived in the diegetic space of the film, figures as the central nervous system from which an assemblage of corporeal, architectural, and social attachments are laterally connected. Relationality in this space entails the easy coupling and decoupling of attachments, hence inverting and resisting the ideological homogenization of time and space in mainstream heterosexual life. Sin Sin Hotel is, therefore, a single node in a larger nodal system, which feeds into the core nervous center that is Bugis Street. The prostitutes and their clients use Bugis Street as the point of initial interface and then move into the hotel, as the street's extension, to reconnect sexually. Foucault also characterizes heterotopias as "most often linked to slices in time" (Foucault 1986, 26). The slicing of time involves capturing individuals within moments in space. These individuals may couple and decouple in different permutations.[5] The film presents a sequence where, after she first arrived at the hotel, Lian learns the various aspects of her job as hotel wait-staff and receptionist,

---

4. While Fruit Chan was working on the screenplay, Yonfan had him lodged at Sin Sin Hotel, an actual third-rate hotel in Singapore (Yonfan 2015, 29).

5. Sophia Siddique visualizes this hotel/brothel as "a site where the dichotomies of sex and gender are dissolved to reveal the interstitial space of liminality. In this site, space and time can no longer be effectively coded in terms of gender division and the demarcation of public and private space. The private or residential space of the bedroom becomes the public site of work and com- modification through the act of prostitution" (1999/2000, 85).

explores every nook and cranny of the building, and gets acquainted with its inhabitants. In narrating the process of Lian's enculturation into Sin Sin Hotel, Yonfan gives us slices in time where Lian faces an aggressive Linda, meets the friendly Lola, remains unfazed by Mr. Wong's verbal abuse, and faints when Mrs. Hwee's son eats a cockroach. Matching these daylight moments of her experience are the equally bizarre nighttime occurrences where the prostitutes appear one by one with their male clientele in tow. The film's noir-ish saxophone soundtrack, together with the ticking grandfather clock, adds sonic texture to these temporal slices, infusing them with a libidinal charge that loosely holds all these moments together into a moving tableau of different human personalities connecting in queer space. It is critical here to note, too, that the film's production of this fluid matrix of space-time connections has an impact on both Lian's and the audience's psychological experience of the diegetic and filmic spaces respectively. The slices in time induce a perceptual friction, what Fran Martin might describe as "temporal dysphoria," which she defines as "a disorientation . . . analogous to motion-sickness (time-sickness?) that is a subjective effect of the regime of cultural time-lag," a concept that "underlines the enduring effects of the former, strongly hierarchized relations between centre and periphery" (Martin 2003a). Hence, the spectral encounters that Lian (and the audience) has with the various denizens of Sin Sin Hotel, as these inhabitants float through its heterotopic spaces, have playfully discombobulating effects. This temporal dysphoria registers both the oppressive power dynamics Bugis Street as cultural space is subjected to, and the tactical power of abject resistance Bugis Street can reclaim as heterotopia.

To illustrate this temporal-spatial atmospheric in the film's heterotopic representations, I turn first to one of my favorite minor characters, the aloof and divinely transcendent Dr. Toh. Lian first meets him when he is dressed as a man; but the next time she sees

Dr. Toh, he surprises both Lian and the viewer with his ethereal and fairy-like persona and outfit: platinum blonde wig, silver white dress, and a translucent sash he sweeps with effortless panache. His ironic comments to Lian frequently leave her baffled and mystified, leading her to believe that he is *"xiao ding dong"*—a Singaporean expression to describe one who is crazy. Accompanying his three appearances in this queer figuration is a musical theme or motif, which sounds impressionist and fluid, akin to Claude Debussy's *Prélude à l'après-midi d'un faune* (1892). Dr. Toh floats on the watery sound, while sashaying effortlessly along the corridors and up and down the stairs. His presence is divine, ghostlike even, imbuing Sin Sin Hotel as a heterotopic space of phantasmagoric haunting.

Figure 6   *Bugis Street* (dir. Yonfan, 1995), the ethereal Dr. Toh

One is reminded of Shakespeare's *A Midsummer Night's Dream* where nymphs and fairies frolic. But more than that, the playful ghostly presence is an ironic commentary on the liminality of embodiment in queer space and time. The divinity-effect, to resurrect Michael Moon's concept here, is also as much a survival tactic as flamboyant personae and outrageous antics are for the transgender.[6]

The scenes with Dr. Toh bring to the film a surrealist quality that produces a queer politics of fantasy and make-believe. Sin Sin Hotel and Bugis Street are spaces where sexual desires and dreams materialize as quickly as they disappear into hellish visions of trauma and horror. In the sequence where the women dress up Lian in the S/M outfit and parade her along Bugis Street, fantasy and reality merge, as temporal and spatial crossings visualize Lian's sexual disorientation. When a fight breaks out between the transgender prostitutes, Lian flees through the seemingly labyrinthine road network surrounding Bugis Street. A blue neon light colors the somnambulistic space, as she runs through an Indian immigrant area, with men leering at her.[7] Lian suddenly hears Zsa Zsa and Sophie screaming away inside the corridor of a darkened shop-house. Zsa Zsa hysterically cries to Lian, "My dreams come true!"—a reference to Zsa Zsa and Sophie's earlier exchange with Lola:

---

6. Dr. Toh's stagey performativity, stereotypical of MTF transgender performances, Yonfan uses again in his campy, melodramatic, ghost story in *Color Blossoms*. Not unlike Dr. Toh, the post-op transsexual diva Madam Satoko Umeki (Keiko Matsuzaka), as a ghostly figure, exudes a mystical aura as she poses and struts, and then suddenly overreacts in classic melodramatic fashion, as Bette Davis would, to the reappearance of her younger male lover Kim (Sho).

7. It is tempting to read this as a racialized moment as the foreign worker population was beginning to grow in the 1990s, though the film is set in the 1960s. Yonfan signals this moment with stereotypical sitar music. What is equally fascinating is the class inflection of these scenes; as prostitutes and foreign workers represent the humanized toll of abjection that mainstream Singaporeans often do not wish to confront in the name of economic progress.

Zsa Zsa: "Girls, girls, girls, I want to be raped tonight by six men."

Sophie: "Quiet! You and I have the same dream."

Lulu: "Don't say so loud. Sure come true. . . ."

Did this gang rape actually take place? If so, why do Zsa Zsa and Sophie, in the next time they appear on screen, seem perfectly unharmed and undisturbed by what must have been a violently traumatizing moment for them? Or, is this rape scene a visual projection of Lian's imagination, informed by her sexual awakening and the earlier conversation the women had with each other? Does ascertaining its reality really matter? My goal in asking these questions is to suggest *Bugis Street* as a cinematic projection of temporal dysphoria in queer heterotopia, where dreams collide with nightmares, pleasure with pain, *jouissance* with trauma, and hope with despair. The blurring division between these opposing concepts helps constitute queer subjectivity, to produce a coping mechanism for survival in a homophobic society that is out to punish, suppress, and even decimate queer sexualities.

The filmic world of *Bugis Street*, therefore, does not romanticize the diegetic Bugis Street as a utopian envisioning of queer historicity, but it instead re-inscribes the space as a heterotopic play on queer affect. It does not shun negativity but embodies a dialectical intersection of good and bad to extol the human frailties and flaws of its subjects. The film is replete with instances of this dynamic at work, many of which I have dealt with in my previous chapter. Where I want to now take this theoretical point, though, is to argue that while the characters' conception of Bugis Street relies on fantasy that at times border on the delusional, the repressed realization of its gritty reality do return and weigh heavily on their consciousness. It is this shuttling between the heights of a paradisiacal vision of Bugis Street and the depths of its grimy day-to-day presence that gives the film its heterotopic nuance.

During their first attempt at sisterly bonding in the kitchen when she teaches Lian French cooking, Drago paints the usual romantic caricature of Paris and interestingly conflates the city with Bugis Street:

> Paris! Oh, Paris! It is the end of dreams for people like us. There is freedom, glamour, spirituality, physicality. And there is this big boulevard called Champs Elysees. And there is Arc de Triomphe. It is L'etoile. The star, it shines so brightly throughout the whole of Paris. Sometimes, when I look at Bugis Street, it reminds me so much of Arc de Triomphe, shining for people like us over the whole of the universe.

Later, when she and Lian visit her mother at the hospital, Drago reflects on her life and career: "I've traveled so widely, done so many things, but somehow I still feel very lost. I spent all my money on expensive clothing and fake jewelry. Not even have enough to stay in a decent hotel. Not that Sin Sin is bad. After all, I'm just a traveling salesman." This discursive shift that we see is not meant to suggest a simplistic binary critique, where because Drago's bombastic conflation of Paris and Bugis Street is delusional, it must be disavowed; and that because her later self-representation as a humble salesman is grounded in reality, it must be embraced. Rather, I view the shift as a discursive flow that spans the political idealism Bugis Street can signify (when Drago interpellates Lian into traversing the disparate spaces of Paris and Bugis Street in order to tease out the ideals of freedom and liberty) and a form of material self-reflection (that criticizes Singapore's consumerist culture, of which Bugis Street is a part). It is queer fantasy that allows Drago to ride this flow, back and forth, and that enables her to deal with the cultural and ideological contradictions Bugis Street embodies. Fantasy, thus, has a major political role to play in configuring the spatial and temporal vectors of queer subjectivity.

Bugis Street as Political Nostalgia and Sentimental Attachments

In his monumental *Theory of Film*, Siegfried Kracauer advocates for "a material aesthetics" that "rests upon the assumption that film is essentially an extension of photography and therefore shares with this medium a marked affinity for the visible world" (Kracauer 1960, xlix). Films draw our attention to the everyday and "the familiar," which "we just take . . . for granted without giving it a thought . . . Films make us undergo similar experiences a thousand times. They alienate our environment in exposing it" (54–55). This process of alienation or estrangement is significant in that it foregrounds not just the texturing of material physicality, which inhabits cinematic space, but it also highlights the spatialization and the embodiment of temporality in often very specific ways:

> The confrontation with objects which are familiar to us for having been part and parcel of our early life is particularly stirring . . . The most familiar, that which continues to condition our involuntary reactions and spontaneous impulses, is thus made to appear as the most alien. If we find these obsolete sights funny, we respond to them also with emotions which range from fright at the sudden emergence of our intimate being to nostalgic melancholy over the inexorable passing of time. (Kracauer 1960, 56–57)[8]

Kracauer identifies a series of filmic modalities to which directors have access in order to produce this effect. For example, "films may cover vast expanses of physical reality" (64), which in the case of *Bugis Street* includes a shot of cloudy skies (which is sonically accompanied by the nostalgic strains of Poon Sow Keng's lovely

---

8. Deleuze makes a similar point about the time-image in his analysis of Ozu's cinematic "still lifes," which he argues are able "to make time and thought perceptible, to make them visible and of sound" (Deleuze 1989, 16–17).

song "情人的眼淚," or "Lover's Tears," at the beginning of the film) and an extreme long shot of a lush garden cove near the hotel with big trees offering a shady canopy (which serves as a geographical signifier for Lian's emotional state, particularly when she requires a sense of comfort). Also, "films may . . . caress one single object long enough to make us imagine its unlimited aspects" (Kracauer 1960, 66), just as *Bugis Street* obsesses over close-up shots of rain water filling a container, a snail creeping along the cement floor, the old grandfather clock ticking in the hotel lobby, and an old-timey radio spewing forth Chinese tunes of the 1950s and 60s. Layering the nostalgic atmosphere of the mise-en-scène is also a yellow coloration that director Yonfan uses to tint the shots of the hotel lobby and Lian's room. In a shot early in the film, the camera pans slowly across Lian's small room to give the viewer a glimpse of the décor and Lian's belongings: glamor shots of Chinese stars, an old-fashion feather duster made of actual rooster feathers, Lian's green dress, a classic electric fan, figurines of Chinese dancers, a red-and-white metal tin cup (which my grandparents also used to own), a small orange-colored table lamp, and a round portable mirror popular among women during the time for make-up purposes.

While the film is clearly trying to be faithful in its representation of the aesthetics of 1960s Singapore, the key question here is: what is the film nostalgic about in its sentimental attachments to these spaces and these objects of the past? Rey Chow's theoretical insights may offer some illumination on this matter:

> [T]he sentimental is thought-provoking not exactly because it allows us to rediscover something old. It is rather that the old, now lingering in the enigmatic form of an intensity (in the form of some emotionally guarded and clung-to inside) that seems neither timely nor fully communicable . . . should nonetheless also be acknowledged as an inherent link to the nexus of becoming visible—in the specific sense of visibility that Deleuze argues. In

other words, more than simply a matter of excavating historical layers of meaning embedded in cinematic images, what I would like to get at is the process in which this . . . epistemic sense of visibility—that is, a trajectory of objectification, recognition, and knowledge that may be made palpable by visual objects such as filmic images but cannot in the end be reduced to them— materializes not only in relation to the visible that is the images but also in the very sentimental interstices—the remains of a collective cultural scaffold—that lend the images their support. (Chow 2007, 23)

What is significant about the visual objectification of these images lies in the relationship between their sentimental intensities and the cultural-political structures in which they are embedded. So, the obvious question in terms of *Bugis Street* is, how is this sentimentalism deployed within the film's queer politics, for the nostalgic imagery is not in itself political or queer? My answer points to the contiguities between fictive and real geographical spaces (an analysis I assume in the next section) and between filmic and discursive temporalities, especially of the political present: in short, the diegetic and meta-filmic contexts. The iconicity of Bugis Street not only as a queer historical past but also as a deterritorialized cultural index of a queer present and future politically energizes these nostalgic images and our sentimental attachments to them. To paraphrase, we imbue these images with political significance on account of the affect they create as we think about them through Bugis Street as queer space and time.

To close this section of the chapter, I want to offer one final example of this queer sentimental attachment to particular props in *Bugis Street*'s mise-en-scène: photographs and posters depicting various famous personalities, and how their diegetic embedding functions in the queer cinematic space of the film. In her analysis of queer spatiality within Tsai Ming-liang's work, Jean Ma observes how his films "confront the viewer with queer appropriations of time and space that unsettle normative understandings of identity and community." Tsai accomplishes this by constructing "a world that is at once familiar and uncanny, fashioned around a realistic iconography of actual, recognizable, and everyday urban locales that are submitted to an operation of defamiliarization" (Ma 2010, 98). One can similarly apply this theoretical lesson about film locations to that of props: the three instances of human portraiture appearing in Lola's room, specifically those of Bruce Lee, Elvis Presley, and Queen Elizabeth II, all of which function as familiar and recognizable imagery during the period. The poster of Bruce Lee is attached to Lola's closet door and its presence is made evident when both the poster and Meng are centered in the frame as Meng rifles through Lola's purse for money. The particular shot, like many others that feature Meng, homoeroticizes his muscular body, which parallels the kind of objectification Bruce Lee, with his exposed torso, experienced as an image of Asian masculine beauty and power. The Bruce Lee poster also happens to function as an interesting temporal marker in the scene's diegetic space. While Jan Uhde and Yvonne Ng Uhde have located the film's setting to be in the 1960s (Uhde and Uhde 2010, 77), it is totally convincing to argue for a 1970s timeframe for the film, since Bruce Lee's career as Hong Kong martial arts icon did not emerge until the 1970s. But this quibble about temporal accuracy is less important than the mode of affective and visual eroticism that the sentimental prop offers within the film's queer space and time. Yonfan admits to Paul Fonoroff in the commentary track to the DVD version that "we did not really say this is exactly which period, but of course it's like 60s during the Vietnam War . . . But in the movie, that we deliberately put some photographs of Teresa Teng . . . and later on you will see there is a poster of Li Xiaolong [Bruce Lee], and things like that," which Fonoroff characterizes as "a mixture of 60s and 70s."⁹ The director gives an explanation for another instance of this temporal displacement in a later work of his:

> There's a film showing within the film [*Prince of Tears*] called "Come Back, My Dear." This film was released in 1958 or 1959 as I recalled, but it appeared in my film, which was supposed to have taken placed in 1954. That's because this was part of my memories. I wouldn't mind if something from 1959 appeared in 1954. As long as I felt it right, then it's right.¹⁰

In other words, the affective power of the image, as it inhabits queer space and travels through queer time, is what matters here.

With an equivalent libidinal inflection to the Bruce Lee poster image, Elvis Presley's photo is framed and hung centered above Lola's dresser. Elvis's gyrating hips pulsate in one's sexual imaginary as Lola makes out with Meng against the dresser. She slaps him, rips off his shirt, kisses him roughly, unzips his pants, pulls down his underwear, and exposes his genitals, all as the King of Rock and Roll regally looks on from above and presides over their passionate interactions. Later, after Lola has parted ways with Meng and has found herself a new boyfriend in Wah Chai, the film offers an equivalent scenic setup between Lola and Wah Chai in front of that same dresser. This time their sexual encounter occurs in the virtual presence of a different but much bigger kind of royalty, a photo portrait of Queen Elizabeth II, which was relatively commonplace in colonial and postcolonial Singapore. Here, the

9. "Director's Conversation with Film Critic Paul Fonoroff," commentary track, Disc One, in *Bugis Street*, dir. Yonfan; perf. Hiep Thi Le, Michael Lam, and David Knight (Hong Kong: Far Sun Film Co. Ltd., 2002), DVD.

10. "Making of *Prince of Tears*," special feature, Disc Two, in *Prince of Tears*, dir. Yonfan; perf. Zhu Xuan, Joseph Chang, Fan Chih-wei (Hong Kong: Far Sun Film Co. Ltd., 2009), DVD.

gendered meaning has definitely been visually transformed. The photo of the British queen resonates with transgender identity and politics in terms of female empowerment.[11] Lola has finally found the emotional strength to rise above her neediness in order to disentangle herself from Meng. Has she learned her lesson about the perils of hitching her wagon to a single male figure? We do not know. But Lola has obviously grown from her experience—as the larger photo of the Queen connotes—and she is wiser from it.

Bugis Street as the Flow of Queer Life

The street as a cinematic space renders time visible through its suggestion of human movement and life passing one by. One of the pleasures of alfresco dining is the visual capturing of life in motion such as people-watching. Pivoting on this visuality is the affinity between the street as a localized space and film as a perfect medium to capture its essence, a concept that Kracauer explains best:

---

11. In the transgender, musical, road-trip classic *The Adventures of Priscilla, Queen of the Desert* (1994), which was released a year before *Bugis Street*, director Stephan Elliot included a shot of Queen Elizabeth II's photo on the wall of a motel room in the Australian Outback, immediately following this monologue that Bernadette (Terence Stamp) addresses to Felicia (Guy Pearce): "It's funny. We all sit around, mindlessly slagging off that vile stink hole of a city. But in some strange way, it takes care of us. I don't know if that ugly world of suburbia has been put there to stop them getting in, or us getting out. Come on. Don't let it drag you down. Let it toughen you up. I can only fight because I've learned to. Being a man one day and a woman the next is not an easy thing to do." *The Adventures of Priscilla, Queen of the Desert* (dir. Stephan Elliot; perf. Terence Stamp, Hugo Weaving, and Guy Pearce [United States: MGM Home Entertainment, 1994], DVD). Whether it is sheer coincidence or that Yonfan is specifically alluding to this moment in Elliot's film, the photo's political resonance for gender politics is unmistakable.

Now films tend to capture physical existence in its endlessness. Accordingly, one may also say that they have an affinity, evidently denied to photography, for the continuum of life or the "flow of life," which of course is identical with open-ended life. The concept "flow of life," then, covers the stream of material situations and happenings with all that they intimate in terms of emotions, values, thoughts. The implication is that the flow of life is predominantly a material rather than a mental continuum, even though, by definition, it extends into the mental dimension . . . The street in the extended sense of the word is not only the arena of fleeting impressions and chance encounters but a place where the flow of life is bound to assert itself. Again one will have to think mainly of the city street with its ever-moving anonymous crowds. The kaleidoscopic sights mingle with unidentified shapes and fragmentary visual complexes and cancel each other out, thereby preventing the onlooker from following up any of the innumerable suggestions they offer. What appears to him are not so much sharp-contoured individuals engaged in this or that definable pursuit as loose throngs of sketchy, completely indeterminate figures. Each has a story, yet the story is not given. Instead, an incessant flow of possibilities and near-intangible meanings appears. This flow casts its spell over the *flâneur* or even creates him. The *flâneur* is intoxicated with life in the street—life eternally dissolving the patterns which it is about to form. (Kracauer 1960, 71–72)

This kaleidoscopic spectacle of incessant movement characterizes the three sequences featuring the film's version of Bugis Street. All three sequences deploy tracking shots to mirror the flow of life, where the transgender prostitutes, foreign sailors, local clients, curious onlookers, and food lovers move in and out, while congregating in a narrow strip of road that is crowded with tables and chairs. The drinking, eating, singing, carousing, flirting, and coupling produce a carnivalesque atmosphere that concretizes in very material ways the rhizomatic assemblage and connectivity

Deleuze and Guattari have theorized. Desire flows as life does in these sequences, a mobility that extends and floods into the spatial confines of Sin Sin Hotel. When the sailors come to town, the Sin Sin prostitutes convey some of them to the hotel lobby. In a wonderful moment in the film, the sailors and the women start dancing, basically turning the lobby into a dance club. Instead of relying on a conventional long shot to capture this visual spectacle, Yonfan chose instead to use a medium close-up, tracking shot of the revelers' feet and then of their mid-sections gyrating to Louis Armstrong's version of "Cabaret." The sensory tectonics of seeing bodies in heat grinding up against each other generate currents of sexual desire that merge into the flow of life.

This flow of queer life that pulses in waves through Sin Sin Hotel and Bugis Street serves as the philosophical foundation for Lola's, and later Lian's, approach to a relational ethics with the Other. In her attempt to lift Lian out of her depressive disposition, Lola redefines love for the sad teenager in the following manner:

> Let me tell you about love. Love is like this hotel. People come in and out all the time. Sometimes there's long-term guests like me. But nothing stays forever. If you're good, they'll come back. If they don't come back, don't worry. It's not because you're bad. Sometimes they just want to try something different.

Despite the imperfections and contradictions in Lola's logic, the depth of her reflection on how life transpires, bringing desire and love with it, indicates the wisdom that comes from her passionate but traumatic experiences with Meng. It is a wisdom that empowers Lola to recalibrate pragmatically her romantic ideals and yet not lose her idealistic hopes and dreams of living a full queer life in Bugis Street. Lola appropriates and transforms the material gaze of the *flâneur* into a philosophy of life that works for her. Eventually catching on to this same philosophy, Lian, in the final scene of the film, pauses meaningfully at the main entrance of the hotel, as she gets ready to set off on her daily trip to the market. Centered in the frame of this exterior shot, she stands upright at attention with her hands clasped in front of her. The background sound features Mrs. Hwee welcoming a new transgender patron, who has just arrived from Bangkok (a signifier of this flow of transnational queer life into Sin Sin Hotel). A smile then suddenly appears on Lian's face and she starts walking briskly and happily again:

> Dear Maria, forget about my last letter. I have to tell you finally I discovered that life is just like our hotel. People come in and out all the time. Sometimes you come across nice clients who treat you really well. And sometimes you have nasty ones who mess up the rooms and take you hours to clean up. But ups and downs, that is what life is promising you.

The imperfections of life, especially with queer life, are what makes it all worth the while. Understanding what this flow of life means will grant one the strength to endure, adapt, and survive. The shot in this final scene concludes with the camera tilting and panning upwards to unveil the hotel rooms and their balconies. The view rotates and turns up and outwards into a crane shot, capturing the street that Sin Sin Hotel is on, before revealing the skyline of Singapore's urban center. As the visual movement of this shot suggests, the microcosmic presence of Sin Sin Hotel and Bugis Street is and will always be a part of Singapore's life stream, both cinematically and discursively.

One final critical gloss on this scene to conclude the chapter: the spatial contiguity between the diegetic Bugis Street and the urban skyline of 1990s Singapore is a fascinating filmic choice, on Yonfan's part, to cross and disrupt spatial and temporal boundaries. All through the film, the director has been very careful to avoid anachronistic slips between the film's 1960s setting and its 1990s

Figure 7 *Bugis Street* (dir. Yonfan, 1995), the film's "Bugis Street" area and the 1990s skyline of Singapore's urban center

production timeframe. The on-location street scenes are carefully composed, often with a low-angle shot, to avoid accidentally capturing on screen contemporary elements. Therefore, for Yonfan now to fracture the seamlessness of *Bugis Street*'s cinematic fantasy through a final cinematographic decision is in itself a calibrated political tactic. As Paul Fonoroff notes in his conversation with Yonfan, "it's like you are deliberately shattering the illusion that you just created of old Singapore. And to do this is very jarring."[12] By conjoining cinematically a 1960s Bugis Street that has disappeared, to a panoramic visual documentation of Singapore's 1990s skyline, Yonfan's film, firstly, registers a visual critique of what the state's urban renewal policies have done to the historical Bugis Street in the past. It sustains that critique by suturing the two slices of time in a single frame and by fixing and maintaining the camera gaze in the shot for a relatively extended period of time before allowing the final fadeout to occur. In arguing that the film "performatively interrogate[s] the notion of linear, ordered, official history by

12. See footnote 9.

presenting a notion of history that contains multiple temporalities and spatialities which exist in radical disjuncture with one another" (Siddique 1999/2000, 87), Sophia Siddique concludes, as I do, that this moment "of permeability and conflation . . . begins to strip away the coherent and linear veneer of official history" (85). Secondly, the ideological goal of drawing the 1990s skyline of Singapore's business district into the film's critique is to signify visually the complicity of the state's economic policy in shoring up transnational corporate interest at the expense of abject minority subcultures, which do not have strong representation or strong voices that demand to be heard. And, finally, one could also argue that Bugis Street, as it has been immortalized through Yonfan's cinematic intervention, is now given renewed political life as a signifier for queer rights in Singapore. The spatial connection on screen between the diegetic Bugis Street to the film's 1990s political present confirms the cultural symbolism of Bugis Street as a queer site of political resistance and futurity.

Conclusion
Bugis Street *as Un-Community*

As I reflect upon the critical trajectory I have taken in analyzing the historical, archival, and filmic discourses of Bugis Street to arrive at some semblance of a theoretical "conclusion"—I dislike the notion of a conclusion in this context, precisely because of its insistent sense of finality, which goes counter to what I see (in hope) as the open-ended potentiality of *Bugis Street*'s political futurity—I keep returning to Maggie Lye, the actress who portrays the character Maggie in the film, as a physical embodiment of Bugis Street in its various incarnations: Maggie was a transsexual sex worker at Bugis Street during its heyday. She returned to work as a customer relations officer in the then newly sanitized iteration of the street, which the state attempted to revive, rather unsuccessfully, in the early 1990s. And, finally, she appears in Yonfan's film as one of the transsexual prostitutes living in Sin Sin Hotel, which, for all intents and purposes, could potentially be read as a fictionalized version of Maggie herself. I had the wonderful privilege and (as a researcher) the good fortune of meeting Maggie and having a conversation with her during one of my trips to Singapore. Generous with her first-hand accounting, Maggie understandably reveals nostalgic longings for Bugis Street in its various permutations, which constitute significant moments in her life. For me, this nostalgia intimates a kind of temporal disjuncture, akin to the temporal dysphoria I discuss in Chapter 4. The slices of personal time that Maggie marries together vibrate anxiously in ethical resonance, to transfigure nostalgia into a form of queer futurity. As she puts it in a local news article about the film:

> I wanted to act in Bugis Street because I thought it would give me a chance to do something for my "*sisters*"—to tell people *our* side of the story . . . But the plot was insubstantial and our roles were shallow . . . The audience may be misled into thinking there is no depth in *our lives* . . . Who knows how many heartaches *we* have suffered? How much ridicule *we* have to put up with? (Koh 1995, 24; emphasis mine)

As my readings in this book reveal, I do not fully agree with Maggie's interpretation of the film. However, I do see in her statement, and in her personal communication to me, a rich understanding of ethical and political outreach and connectivity to her "sisters" as a communal "we," which I seek to honor here. But who is this "we," who are her "sisters"? I want to offer a more expansive and inclusive reading of this plural first-person personal pronoun, as a "we" that transcends historical specificity by synaptically leaping across temporal and cultural zones. It is a communalism that circumnavigates the problematic constraints and restraints of Community, with a capital "C." It is, I theorize, a form of queer "un-community," connecting those who are queerly *un*common and those who queerly *dis*identify.

My analysis of cultural anxiety over Bugis Street, the shifting fabulations in its pop cultural archive, the disidentificatory queer politics of Yonfan's transnational film, and the cinematic projection of Bugis Street as queer space and time can be similarly summed up as a politics of "un-community." Italian philosopher Roberto Esposito has warned us of the burdens that community, as an ideological construct, imposes on us and what that burden can result in, in terms of the political subject, and the rights and freedoms to which it is entitled. Esposito draws from the etymology of the Latin word *communitas* to arrive at the following theoretical conclusion about community: "The subjects of community are united by an 'obligation,' in the sense that we say 'I owe *you* something,' but not 'you owe *me* something.' This is what makes them not less than the masters of themselves, and that more precisely expropriates them of their initial property (in part or completely), of the most proper property, namely, their very subjectivity." Esposito further argues that community should not "be interpreted as a mutual, intersubjective 'recognition' in which individuals are reflected in each other so as to confirm their initial identity," but is a coercive structure that induces "a spasm in the continuity of the subject" (Esposito 2010, 6–7). In the same vein, Judith Halberstam's contention "that quests for community are always nostalgic attempts to return to some fantasized moment of union and unity reveals the conservative stakes in community for all kinds of political projects, and makes the reconsideration of subcultures all the more urgent" (Halberstam 2005, 154). Therefore, for queer activism to be true to its queerness, one must continue to be watchful of the urge to embrace community in its clarion call to an imagined queer utopia of cultural homogeneity. So, instead of the more categorical and binary-inducing "anti-community," I have opted for the neologistic formulation "un-community" to articulate Esposito's suggestion that we "immunize" ourselves against the ideological pressures of community, "to negate the very same foundations of community"

(Esposito 2010, 13), without sacrificing the political possibilities and necessities of relating and connecting to one another.[1]

Yonfan's *Bugis Street* as a political project of filmic intervention challenges the interpellative call to return to normative community, a community that once rejected the transgender and sexual alterities of Bugis Street, forcibly erased them from its social map, and suppressed their discursive presence through various modes of censorship. The flow of life in queer time and space that the film envisions circumscribes the essentializing strictures of community, even queer community. *Bugis Street*, hence, forces viewers to think differently about an ethics of relationality, in the hope that queer activism in Singapore, and around the world, can more effectively combat the imperatives of heteronormativity and resist the temptations that the assimilationist logics of homonormativity pose. Or, as Leo Bersani so elegantly puts it, "*homo-ness itself necessitates a massive redefining of relationality* . . . There are some glorious precedents for thinking of homosexuality as truly disruptive—as a *force* not limited to the modest goals of tolerance for diverse lifestyles, but in fact mandating the politically unacceptable and politically indispensable choice of an outlaw existence" (Bersani 1995, 76). Only then can a truly egalitarian space and time be found for queer individuals of all stripes and colors.

---

1. Halberstam's "subcultures" seem to suggest this alternative construction to community that I am positing.

Credits

Bugis Street (妖街皇后)

Singapore / Hong Kong 1995

Director
Yonfan

Producer
Katy Yew

Executive Producer
Godfrey Yew

Screenplay
Fruit Chan
Yonfan

Director of Photography
Jacky Tang

Editor
Kam Ma

Art Director
Ma Man Ming

Music Dircctor
Chris Babida

Production Company
Jaytex Productions Pte. Ltd.

Production Manager
Willis Lee

Line Producer
Daniel Yu

Sound Recordist
Sharman Lee

Costumes
Cynthia Lim
Julian Tok

Make-Up Artists
Anuar
Mindy Ho

Cast
Hiep Thi Le, as Lian
Michael Lam, as Meng
Benedict Goh, as Sing
Greg-O, as Drago
Ernest, as Lola
David Knight, as Sailor
Maggie Lye, as Maggie
Gerald Chen, as Mrs. Hwee
Mavia, as Zsa Zsa

Sofia, as Sophie
Linden, as Linda
Matthew Foo, as Dr. Toh
Godfrey Yew, as Mr. Wong
Sim Boon Peng, as Ah Kit
Charles, as Wah Chai
Lily Ong, as Drago's Mother

Duration
105 minutes

Color

Languages
In Chinese, English, and Singlish, with Chinese and English subtitles

Yonfan's Filmography

A Certain Romance (少女日記), 1984.

The Story of Rose (玫瑰的故事), 1985.

Immortal Story (海上花), 1986.

Double Fixation (意亂情迷), 1987.

Last Romance (流金歲月), 1988.

Promising Miss Bowie (祝福), 1990.

In Between (新同居時代), with Sylvia Chang and Leung Chun Chiu, 1994.

Bugis Street (妖街皇后), 1995.

Bishonen (美少年の戀), 1998.

Peony Pavilion (遊園驚夢), 2001.

Breaking the Willow (鳳冠情事), 2003.

Color Blossoms (桃色), 2004.

Prince of Tears (淚王子), 2009.

General Filmography

15, Royston Tan, 2003.

2000 AD (公元 2000), Gordon Chan, 2000.

The Adventures of Priscilla, Queen of the Desert, Stephan Elliott, 1994.

American Pie, Paul Weitz, 1999.

Army Daze, Ong Keng Sen, 1996.

Around the World in 80 Days, Frank Coraci, 2004.

Ashes of Time (東邪西毒), Wong Kar-wai, 1994.

A Better Tomorrow (英雄本色), John Woo, 1986.

The Blue Lagoon, Randal Kleiser, 1980.

Brokeback Mountain, Ang Lee, 2005.

Carrie, Brian De Palma, 1976.

The Celluloid Closet, Rob Epstein and Jeffrey Friedman, 1995.

A Chinese Ghost Story (倩女幽魂), Ching Siu-tung, 1987.

Durian Durian (榴槤飄飄), Fruit Chan, 2000.

Farewell My Concubine (霸王別姬), Chen Kaige, 1993.

Forever Fever, Glen Goei, 1998.

The Girlie Bar (酒簾), John Lo Ma, 1976.

The Goddess (神女), Wu Yonggang, 1934.

The Graduate, Mike Nichols, 1967.

Happy Together (春光乍洩), Wong Kar-wai, 1997.

The Hawaiians, Tom Gries, 1970.

Heaven and Earth, Oliver Stone, 1993.

Hollywood Hong-Kong (香港有個荷里活), Fruit Chan, 2001.

House of Fury (精武家庭), Stephen Fung, 2005.

Intimate Confessions of a Chinese Courtesan (愛奴), Chor Yuen, 1972.

Juno, Jason Reitman, 2007.

Kiss of Death (毒女), Ho Meng-hua, 1973.

Lan Yu (藍宇), Stanley Kwan, 2001.

Liang Po Po: The Movie (梁婆婆重出江湖), Teng Bee Lian, 1999.

The Love Eterne (梁山伯與祝英台), Li Han-hsiang, 1963.

Love Is a Many-Splendored Thing, Henry King, 1955.

The Lovers (梁祝), Tsui Hark, 1994.

Lust for Love of a Chinese Courtesan (愛奴新傳), Chor Yuen, 1984.

Made in Hong Kong (香港製造), Fruit Chan, 1997.

M*A*S*H, Robert Altman, 1970.

Mee Pok Man, Eric Khoo, 1996.

Money No Enough (錢不夠用), Jack Neo, 1998.

Moonrise Kingdom, Wes Anderson, 2012.

Mrs. Doubtfire, Chris Columbus, 1993.

Peking Opera Blues (刀馬旦), Tsui Hark, 1986.

Perth, Djinn, 2004.

Pleasure Factory, Ekachai Uekrongtham, 2007.

Porky's, Bob Clark, 1982.

Protégé (門徒), Derek Yee, 2007.

Queen of Temple Street (廟街皇后), Lawrence Ah Mon, 1990.

Return to Pontianak, Djinn, 2001.

The Rocky Horror Picture Show, Jim Sharman, 1975.

Saint Jack, Peter Bogdanovich, 1979.

Sayonara, Joshua Logan, 1957.

Sex for Sale (面具), Chang Tseng-chai, 1974.

A Single Man, Tom Ford, 2009.

Solos, Kan Lume and Loo Zihan, 2007.

Some Like It Hot, Billy Wilder, 1959.

The Sugar Daddies (桃色經濟), Sun Chung, 1973.

Swordsman II (笑傲江湖之東方不敗), Ching Siu-tung, 1992.

Swordsman III: The East Is Red (東方不敗：風雲再起), Ching Siu-tung, 1993.

Tai Chi Hero (太極2：英雄崛起), Stephen Fung, 2012.

Talking Cock the Movie, Colin Goh and Yen Yen Woo, 2002.

To Wong Foo, Thanks for Everything! Julie Newmar, Beeban Kidron, 1995.

Tootsie, Sydney Pollack, 1982.

Untitled, Loo Zihan, 2005.

The Wedding Banquet, Ang Lee, 1993.

Women of Desire (女人面面觀), Lui Kay, 1974.

Women Who Love Women, Lim May Ling, 2006.

The World of Suzie Wong, Richard Quine, 1960.

Yang ± Yin: Gender in Chinese Cinema (男生女相：華語電影之性別), Stanley Kwan, 1998.

The Young Girls of Rochefort (*Les demoiselles de Rochefort*), Jacques Demy, 1967.

Bibliography

Agamben, Giorgio. 2011. *Nudities*, translated by David Kishik and Stefan Pedatella. Stanford: Stanford University Press.

Ang, Ien. 2001. *On Not Speaking Chinese: Living Between Asia and the West*. London: Routledge.

Au, Alex. 2002. The Leech on the Trannie's Bum. *Yawning Bread*, accessed September 28, 2012, http://www.yawningbread.org/arch_2002/yax-276.htm.

Baker, Jim. 2008. *Crossroads: A Popular History of Malaysia and Singapore*. Singapore: Marshall Cavendish.

Barnes, Julian. 1989. *A History of the World in 10½ Chapters*. New York: Vintage International.

Berry, Chris. 2000. Happy Alone? Sad Young Men in East Asian Gay Cinema. In *Queer Asian Cinema: Shadows in the Shade*, edited by Andrew Grossman, 187–200. New York: Harrington Park Press.

———. 2001. Asian Values, Family Values: Film, Video, and Lesbian and Gay Identities. In *Gay and Lesbian Asia: Culture, Identity, Community*, edited by Gerard Sullivan and Peter A. Jackson, 211–31. New York: Harrington Park Press.

———. 2011. Transnational Chinese Cinema Studies. In *The Chinese Cinema Book*, edited by Song Hwee Lim and Julian Ward, 9–16. London: BFI / Palgrave Macmillan.

Berry, Chris, and Mary Farquhar. 2006. *China on Screen: Cinema and Nation*. Hong Kong: Hong Kong University Press.

Bersani, Leo. 1995. *Homos*. Cambridge, MA. Harvard University Press.

Bhabha, Homi K. 1994. *The Location of Culture*. London: Routledge.

Blackwood, Evelyn. 2005. Gender Transgression in Colonial and Postcolonial Indonesia. *The Journal of Asian Studies* 64 (4): 849–79.

Bob from Australia. 2002. The Sailor's Birthday Present. *Yawning Bread*, accessed January 4, 2013, http://www.yawningbread.org/guest_2002/guw-078.htm.

Bobel, Chris. 2010. *New Blood: Third-Wave Feminism and the Politics of Menstruation*. New Brunswick: Rutgers University Press.

Browne, Nick, Paul G. Pickowicz, Vivian Sobchack, and Esther Yau, eds. 1994. *New Chinese Cinemas: Forms, Identities, Politics*. Cambridge: Cambridge University Press.

Chan, Kenneth. 2004. Cross-Dress for Success: Performing Ivan Heng and Chowee Leow's *An Occasional Orchid* and Stella Kon's *Emily of Emerald Hill* on the Singapore Stage. *Tulsa Studies in Women's Literature* 23 (1): 29–43.

———. 2008. Tactics of Tears: Excess/Erasure in the Gay Chinese Melodramas of *Fleeing by Night* and *Lan Yu*. *Camera Obscura* 68, Vol. 23 (2): 141–66.

———. 2009. *Remade in Hollywood: The Global Chinese Presence in Transnational Cinemas*. Hong Kong: Hong Kong University Press.

———. 2012. Impossible Presence: Toward a Queer Singapore Cinema, 1990s–2000s. In *Queer Singapore: Illiberal Citizenship and Mediated Cultures*, edited by Audrey Yue and Jun Zubillaga-Pow, 161–74. Hong Kong: Hong Kong University Press.

Chauncey, George. 2009. The Trouble with Shame. In *Gay Shame*, edited by David M. Halperin and Valerie Traub, 277–82. Chicago: The University of Chicago Press.

Chou Wah-shan. 2000. *Tongzhi: Politics of Same-Sex Eroticism in Chinese Societies*. New York: Haworth Press.

Chow, Rey. 1998. *Ethics after Idealism: Theory-Culture-Ethnicity-Reading*. Bloomington: Indiana University Press.

———. 2007. *Sentimental Fabulations, Contemporary Chinese Films: Attachment in the Age of Global Visibility*. New York: Columbia University Press.

Chu, Karen. 2011a. Busan International Film Festival to Feature Yonfan Retrospective. *The Hollywood Reporter*, accessed October 1, 2012, http://www.hollywoodreporter.com/news/busan-international-film-festival-feature-231299.

———. 2011b. Hong Kong Auteur Yonfan Relishes His Role as Talent Scout. *The Hollywood Reporter*, accessed October 1, 2012, http://www.hollywoodreporter.com/news/hong-kong-auteur-yonfan-relishes-245068.

Chua Beng-Huat. 1997. *Political Legitimacy and Housing: Stakeholding in Singapore*. London: Routledge.

Chua, Lynette J. 2014. *Mobilizing Gay Singapore: Rights and Resistance in an Authoritarian State*. Philadelphia: Temple University Press.

Chung, Stephanie, Po-yin. 2003. The Industrial Evolution of a Fraternal Enterprise: The Shaw Brothers and the Shaw Organisation. In *The Shaw Screen: A Preliminary Study*, edited by Wong Ain-ling, 1–17. Hong Kong: Hong Kong Film Archive.

Coonan, Clifford. 2011. Asian Film Noms Announced. *Variety*, accessed October 1, 2012, http://www.variety.com/article/VR1118030593/.

Davies, Sharyn Graham. 2007. *Challenging Gender Norms: Five Genders among the Bugis in Indonesia*. Belmont, CA: Thomson Wadsworth.

Deleuze, Gilles. 1989. *Cinema 2: The Time-Image*, translated by Hugh Tomlinson and Robert Galeta. London: Continuum.

Deleuze, Gilles, and Félix Guattari. 1983. *Anti-Oedipus: Capitalism and Schizophrenia*, translated by Robert Hurley, Mark Seem, and Helen R. Lane. Minneapolis: University of Minnesota.

———. 1987. *A Thousand Plateaus: Capitalism and Schizophrenia*, translated by Brian Massumi. Minneapolis: University of Minnesota.

Derrida, Jacques. 1995. *Archive Fever: A Freudian Impression*, translated by Eric Prenowitz. Chicago: The University of Chicago Press.

Doane, Mary Ann. 2002. *The Emergence of Cinematic Time: Modernity, Contingency, The Archive*. Cambridge, MA: Harvard University Press.

Dyer, Richard. 2002. *The Culture of Queers*. London: Routledge.

Eckardt, James. 2006. *Singapore Girl: A True Story of Sex, Drugs and Love on the Wild Side in 1970s Bugis Street*. Singapore: Monsoon Books. Kindle edition.

Esposito, Roberto. 2010. *Communitas: The Origin and Destiny of Community*, translated by Timothy Campbell. Stanford: Stanford University Press.

Foucault, Michel. 1978. *The History of Sexuality: Volume 1: An Introduction*, translated by Robert Hurley. New York: Vintage Books.

———. 1986. Of Other Spaces, translated by Jay Miskowiec. *Diacritics* 16 (1): 22–27.

Freeman, Elizabeth. 2010. *Time Binds: Queer Temporalities, Queer Histories*. Durham: Duke University Press. Kindle edition.

Fujii, Tatsuki. 1994. The Japanese Journalist. In *Travellers' Singapore: An Anthology*, edited by John Bastin, 239–42. Oxford: Oxford University Press.

Garber, Marjorie. 1992. *Vested Interests: Cross-Dressing and Cultural Anxiety*. New York: Routledge.

Gawthrop, Daniel. 2005. *The Rice Queen Diaries: A Memoir*. Vancouver: Arsenal Pulp Press.

Groppe, Alison M. 2014. "Singlish" and the Sinophone: Nonstandard (Chinese/English) Languages in Recent Singaporean Cinema. In *Sinophone Cinemas*, edited by Audrey Yue and Olivia Khoo, 147–68. New York: Palgrave Macmillan.

Grosz, Elizabeth. 1994. *Volatile Bodies: Toward a Corporeal Feminism*. Bloomington: Indiana University Press.

Halberstam, Judith. 2005. *In a Queer Time and Place: Transgender Bodies, Subcultural Lives*. New York: New York University Press.

Halperin, David M., and Valerie Traub, eds. 2009. *Gay Shame*. Chicago: The University of Chicago Press.

Hanson, Ellis. 2009. Teaching Shame. In *Gay Shame*, edited by David M. Halperin and Valerie Traub, 132–64. Chicago: The University of Chicago Press.

Harris, Kristine. 2008. *The Goddess*: Fallen Woman of Shanghai. In *Chinese Films in Focus II*, edited by Chris Berry, 128–36. New York: BFI/Palgrave Macmillan.

Heng, Russell, Hiang Khng. 2001. Tiptoe Out of the Closet: The Before and After of the Increasingly Visible Gay Community in Singapore. In *Gay and Lesbian Asia: Culture, Identity, Community*, edited by Gerard Sullivan and Peter A. Jackson, 81–97. New York: Harrington Park Press.

Higbee, Will, and Song Hwee Lim. 2010. Concepts of Transnational Cinema: Towards a Critical Transnationalism in Film Studies. *Transnational Cinemas* 1(1): 7–21.

Ho, Jason, Ka-Hang. 2012. A Chinese Queer Discourse: Camp and Alternative Desires in the Films of Yon Fan and Lou Ye. In *LGBT Transnational Identity and the Media*, edited by Christopher Pullen, 290–307. New York: Palgrave Macmillan.

Hor, Michael. 2012. Enforcement of 377A: Entering the Twilight Zone. In *Queer Singapore: Illiberal Citizenship and Mediated Cultures*, edited by Audrey Yue and Jun Zubillaga-Pow, 45–58. Hong Kong: Hong Kong University Press.

Hwang, David Henry. 1988. *M. Butterfly*. New York: Dramatists Play Service Inc.

Jackson, Peter A. 2001. Pre-Gay, Post-Queer: Thai Perspectives on Proliferating Gender/Sex Diversity in Asia. In *Gay and Lesbian Asia: Culture, Identity, Community*, edited by Gerard Sullivan and Peter A. Jackson, 1–25. New York: Harrington Park Press.

Kaye, Barrington. 1955. *Bugis Street Blues: A Sentimental Guide to Singapore*. Singapore: Donald Moore.

Kingston, Maxine Hong. 1976. *The Woman Warrior: Memoirs of a Girlhood among Ghosts*. New York: Vintage International.

Kinsey, Alfred C., Wardell B. Pomeroy, and Clyde E. Martin. 1998. *Sexual Behavior in the Human Male*. Bloomington: Indiana University Press.

Koh Buck Song, with Tan Hwee Hua. 1994. *Bugis Street: The Novel*. Singapore: Pacific Theatricals.

Koh, Maureen. 1995. "We Were Exploited." *New Paper*, April 27: 24.

Kong, Travis S. K. 2005. Queering Masculinity in Hong Kong Movies. In *Masculinities and Hong Kong Cinema*, edited by Laikwan Pang and Day Wong, 57–80. Hong Kong: Hong Kong University Press.

Kozlov, Vladimir. 2012. Moscow Int'l Film Fest to Kick Off on June 21.

The Hollywood Reporter, accessed October 1, 2012, http://www. hollywoodreporter.com/news/moscow-intl-film-fest-kick-339050.

Kracauer, Siegfried. 1960. *Theory of Film: The Redemption of Physical Reality*. Princeton: Princeton University Press.

Kwan Chooi Tow. 1992. Bugis St Gets Transsexuals to Be Customer Relations Officers. *Straits Times*, April 20.

Leung, Helen Hok-Sze. 2005. Unsung Heroes: Reading Transgender Subjectivities in Hong Kong Action Cinema. In *Masculinities and Hong Kong Cinema*, edited by Laikwan Pang and Day Wong, 81–98. Hong Kong: Hong Kong University Press.

———. 2008. *Undercurrents: Queer Culture and Postcolonial Hong Kong*. Vancouver: UBC Press.

———. 2010. *Farewell My Concubine: A Queer Film Classic*. Vancouver: Arsenal Pulp Press.

———. 2012. Trans on Screen. In *Transgender China*, edited by Howard Chiang, 183–98. New York: Palgrave Macmillan.

Li, John. 2010. Yonfan–An Artist of the World. *movieXclusive.com*, accessed December 13, 2012, http://www.moviexclusive.com/article/yonfananartistoftheworld/yonfananartistoftheworld.html.

Lim, Gerrie. 2004. *Invisible Trade: High-Class Sex for Sale in Singapore*. Singapore: Monsoon Books.

Lim, Song Hwee. 2006. *Celluloid Comrades: Representations of Male Homosexuality in Contemporary Chinese Cinemas*. Honolulu: University of Hawai'i Press.

———. 2007. Is the Trans-in Transnational the Trans-in Transgender? *New Cinemas: Journal of Contemporary Film* 5 (1): 39–52.

———. 2011. Six Chinese Cinemas in Search of a Historiography. In *The Chinese Cinema Book*, edited by Song Hwee Lim and Julian Ward, 35–43. London: BFI / Palgrave Macmillan.

———. 2014. The Voice of the Sinophone. In *Sinophone Cinemas*, edited by Audrey Yue and Olivia Khoo, 62–76. New York: Palgrave Macmillan.

Lo, Joseph, and Huang Guoqin, eds. 2003. *People Like Us: Sexual Minorities in Singapore*. Singapore: Select Publishing.

Lo, Kwai-Cheung. 2005. *Chinese Face/Off: The Transnational Popular Culture of Hong Kong*. Urbana: University of Illinois Press.

Louie, Kam. 2002. *Theorising Chinese Masculinity: Society and Gender in China*. Cambridge: Cambridge University Press.

Lu, Sheldon Hsiao-peng. 1997a. Historical Introduction: Chinese Cinemas (1896–1996) and Transnational Film Studies. In *Transnational Chinese Cinemas: Identity, Nationhood, Gender*, edited by Sheldon Hsiao-peng Lu, 1–31. Honolulu: University of Hawai'i Press.

———, ed. 1997b. *Transnational Chinese Cinemas: Identity, Nationhood, Gender*. Honolulu: University of Hawai'i Press.

Lu, Sheldon H. 2014. Genealogies of Four Critical Paradigms in Chinese-Language Film Studies. In *Sinophone Cinemas*, edited by Audrey Yue and Olivia Khoo, 13–25. New York: Palgrave Macmillan.

Lu, Sheldon H., and Emilie Yueh-yu Yeh, eds. 2005. *Chinese-Language Film: Historiography, Poetics, Politics*. Honolulu: University of Hawai'i Press.

Ma, Jean. 2010. *Melancholy Drift: Marking Time in Chinese Cinema*. Hong Kong: Hong Kong University Press. Kindle edition.

Marchetti, Gina. 1993. *Romance and the "Yellow Peril": Race, Sex, and Discourse Strategies in Hollywood Fiction*. Berkeley: University of California Press.

———. 2006. *From Tian'anmen to Times Square: Transnational China and the Chinese Diaspora on Global Screens, 1989–1997*. Philadelphia: Temple University Press.

Martin, Fran. 2003a. The European Undead: Tsai Ming-liang's Temporal Dysphoria. *Senses of Cinema*, 27. Accessed November 10, 2013, http://sensesofcinema.com/2003/feature-articles/tsai_european_undead/.

———. 2003b. *Situating Sexualities: Queer Representation in Taiwanese Fiction, Film, and Public Culture*. Hong Kong: Hong Kong University Press.

———. 2010. *Backward Glances: Contemporary Chinese Cultures and the Female Homoerotic Imaginary*. Durham: Duke University Press.

Millar, Susan Bolyard. 1983. On Interpreting Gender in Bugis Society. *American Ethnologist* 10 (3): 477–93.

Millet, Raphaël. 2006. *Singapore Cinema*. Singapore: Editions Didier Miller.

Moon, Michael, and Eve Kosofsky Sedgwick. 2001. Divinity: A Dossier, a Performance Piece, a Little-Understood Emotion. In *Bodies Out of*

Bounds: Fatness and Transgression, edited by Jana Evans Braziel and Kathleen LeBesco, 292–328. Berkeley: University of California Press.

Morris, Meaghan, Siu Leung Li, and Stephen Chan Ching-kiu, eds. 2005. *Hong Kong Connections: Transnational Imagination in Action Cinema*. Durham: Duke University Press.

Mulvey, Laura. 1992. Visual Pleasure and Narrative Cinema. In *The Sexual Subject: A* Screen *Reader in Sexuality*, edited by *Screen* editors, 22–34. London: Routledge.

Muñoz, José Esteban. 1999. *Disidentifications: Queers of Color and the Performance of Politics*. Minneapolis: University of Minnesota Press.

Ng, Thomas. 2003. Law and Homosexuals. In *People Like Us: Sexual Minorities in Singapore*, edited by Joseph Lo and Huang Guoqin, 17–20. Singapore: Select Publishing.

Ommanney, F. D. 1962. *Eastern Windows*. London: Readers Union.

Puar, Jasbir K. 2007. *Terrorist Assemblages: Homonationalism in Queer Times*. Durham: Duke University Press.

Rodowick. D. N. 2007. *The Virtual Life of Film*. Cambridge, MA: Harvard University Press, 2007.

Rosewarne, Lauren. 2012. *Periods in Pop Culture: Menstruation in Film and Television*. Lanham, MD: Lexington Books.

Russo, Vito. 1987. *The Celluloid Closet: Homosexuality in the Movies*. Revised edition. New York: Harper & Row.

Sa'at, Alfian Bin. 2012. Hinterland, Heartland, Home: Affective Topography in Singapore Films. In *Southeast Asian Independent Cinema*, edited by Tilman Baumgärtel, 33–50. Hong Kong: Hong Kong University Press.

Said, Edward W. 1978. *Orientalism*. New York: Vintage Books.

———. 1993. *Culture and Imperialism*. New York: Vintage Books.

Sedgwick, Eve Kosofsky. 1985. *Between Men: English Literature and Male Homosocial Desire*. New York: Columbia University Press.

———. 1990. *Epistemology of the Closet*. Berkeley: University of California Press.

Shih, Shu-mei. 2007. *Visuality and Identity: Sinophone Articulations across the Pacific*. Berkeley: University of California Press.

Siddique, Sophia. 1999/2000. Performing Cultural Memory in Singapore. *Spectator: The University of Southern California Journal of Film and Television* 20 (1): 77–89.

Slater, Ben. 2013. Coming of Age: "Hollywood" in Singapore: Pt. 1: Pretty Polly AKA A Matter of Innocence, Guy Green, 1967/1968. Accessed January 27, 2015, http://sporeana.blogspot.sg/2013/05/coming-of-age-hollywood-arrives-in.html.

———. 2014. Pretty Polly AKA A Matter of Innocence (1967). In *World Film Locations: Singapore*, edited by Lorenzo Codelli, 48–49. Bristol, UK: Intellect.

Stryker, Susan. 2006. (De)Subjugated Knowledges: An Introduction to Transgender Studies. In *The Transgender Studies Reader*, edited by Susan Stryker and Stephen Whittle, 1–17. New York: Routledge.

Szeto, Mirana M. 2014. Sinophone Libidinal Economy in the Age of Neoliberalization and Mainlandization: Masculinities in Hong Kong SAR New Wave Cinema. In *Sinophone Cinemas*, edited by Audrey Yue and Olivia Khoo, 120–46. New York: Palgrave Macmillan.

Tan, Chris K. K. 2012. "Oi, Recruit! Wake Up Your Idea!": Homosexuality and Cultural Citizenship in the Singapore Military. In *Queer Singapore: Illiberal Citizenship and Mediated Cultures*, edited by Audrey Yue and Jun Zubillaga-Pow, 71–81. Hong Kong: Hong Kong University Press.

Tan, Kenneth Paul. 2008. *Cinema and Television in Singapore: Resistance in One Dimension.* Leiden, the Netherlands: Brill.

Tan, Roy. Bugis Street: Transgender Aspects. *Singapore LGBT Encyclopedia*, accessed January 23, 2015, http://sporelgbtpedia.shoutwiki.com/wiki/Bugis_Street:_transgender_aspects.

———. 2012. Photo Essay: A Brief History of Early Gay Venues in Singapore. In *Queer Singapore: Illiberal Citizenship and Mediated Cultures*, edited by Audrey Yue and Jun Zubillaga-Pow, 117–47. Hong Kong: Hong Kong University Press.

Tan See Kam. 2013. Memorialization, Melancholia and Melancholizing in Shaw Brothers' *Fengyue* (Erotic) Films. *Screen* 54 (1): 82–103.

Tan See-Kam and Annette Aw. 2008. *The Love Eterne*: Almost a (Heterosexual) Love Story. In *Chinese Films in Focus II*, edited by Chris Berry, 160–66. New York: Palgrave Macmillan.

Teo, Stephen. 1997. *Hong Kong Cinema: The Extra Dimension*. London: BFI.

——. 2009. *Chinese Martial Arts Cinema: The* Wuxia *Tradition*. Edinburgh: Edinburgh University Press.

THR Staff. 2011. Chinese Director Yonfan to Head Up Busan New Currents Jury. *The Hollywood Reporter*, accessed October 1, 2012, http://www. hollywoodreporter.com/news/chinese-director-yonfan-head-up-225872.

Thulaja, Naidu Ratnala. 2010. Film Classification for Restriction [Restricted (Artistic) Category]. *Singapore Infopedia*, accessed January 27, 2015, http://eresources.nlb.gov.sg/infopedia/articles/SIP_15_2004–12-27.html.

Travis, Alan. 2002. Navy Chiefs Ordered Secret Purge of Gay Sailors. *The Guardian*, accessed May 12, 2011, http://www.guardian.co.uk/uk/2002/oct/31/military.gayrights.

Turnbull, C. M. 2009. *A History of Modern Singapore: 1819–2005*. Singapore: NUS Press.

Uhde, Jan, and Yvonne Ng Uhde. 2010. *Latent Images: Film in Singapore*. Second edition. Singapore: Ridge Books.

Valentine, David. 2007. *Imagining Transgender: An Ethnography of a Category*. Durham: Duke University Press.

Warner, Michael. 1999. *The Trouble with Normal: Sex, Politics, and the Ethics of Queer Life*. Cambridge, MA: Harvard University Press.

Warren, James Francis. 2003. Ah Ku *and* Karayuki-san*: Prostitution in Singapore 1870–1940*. Singapore: Singapore University Press.

Wells, Carveth. 1994. Raffles Hotel. In *Travellers' Singapore: An Anthology*, edited by John Bastin, 242–49. Oxford: Oxford University Press.

Williams, Linda. 1989. *Hard Core: Power, Pleasure, and the "Frenzy of the Visible."* Berkeley: University of California Press.

——. 2008. *Screening Sex*. Durham: Duke University Press.

Williams, Tony. 2010. Brigitte Lin Ching Hsia: Last Eastern Star of the Late Twentieth Century. In *Chinese Film Stars*, edited by Mary Farquhar and Yingjin Zhang, 139–50. London: Routledge.

Wong Ain-ling, ed. 2003. *The Shaw Screen: A Preliminary Study*. Hong Kong: Hong Kong Film Archive.

Yau, Esther C. M., ed. 2001. *At Full Speed: Hong Kong Cinema in a Borderless World*. Minneapolis: University of Minnesota Press.

Yeh Yueh-yu. 1998. Defining "Chinese." *Jump Cut: A Review of Contemporary Media* (42): 73–76.

Yeo Toon Joo, Betty L. Khoo, and Lee Chiu San. 1972. They Are Different . . . *New Nation*, July 24: 9.

Yonfan. 1995. *Bugis Street: A Movie Book by Yonfan*. Hong Kong: Far-Sun Film Co. Ltd.

Yonfan (楊凡). 2012. 楊凡時間 (*Intermission*). Hong Kong: Oxford University Press.

———. 2015. 浮花 [Floating flowers]. Hong Kong: Oxford University Press.

Yue, Audrey, and Olivia Khoo, eds. 2014. *Sinophone Cinemas*. New York: Palgrave Macmillan.

Yue, Audrey, and Jun Zubillaga-Pow, eds. 2012. *Queer Singapore: Illiberal Citizenship and Mediated Cultures*. Hong Kong: Hong Kong University Press.

Zhang, Yingjin. 2004. *Chinese National Cinema*. New York: Routledge.